THIS BOOK BELONGS TO
The Library of

....

....

@COPYRIGHT 2024

The content contained within this book may not be reproduced, duplicated, or transmitted without direct written permission from the author or the publisher. Under no circumstances will any blame or legal responsibility be held against the publisher, or author, for any damages, reparation, or monetary loss due to the information contained within this book. Either directly or indirectly.

Legal Notice:

This book is copyright protected. This book is only for personal use. You cannot amend, distribute, sell, use, quote, or paraphrase any part, or the content within this book, without the consent of the author or publisher.

Disclaimer Notice:

Please note the information contained within this document is for educational and entertainment purposes only. All effort has been executed to present accurate, up-to-date, and reliable, complete information. No warranties of any kind are declared or implied. Readers acknowledge that the author is not engaging in the rendering of legal, financial, medical, or professional advice. The content within this book has been derived from various sources. Please consult a licensed professional before attempting any techniques outlined in this book. By reading this document, the reader agrees that under no circumstances is the author responsible for any losses, direct or indirect, which are incurred as a result of the use of the information contained within this document, including, but not limited to — errors, omissions, or inaccuracies.

Thanks ever so much to each of my cherished readers for investing the time to read this book!

I know you could have picked from many other books, but you chose this one. So, a big thanks for reading all the way to the end. If you enjoyed this book or received value from it, I'd like to ask you for a favor. Please take a few minutes to **post an honest and heartfelt review on** *Amazon.com.* Your support does make a difference and helps to benefit other people.

Thanks!

Table of Contents

CHAPTER 1	5
CHAPTER 2	15
PART ONE	23
CHAPTER 3	24
CHAPTER 4	35
PART TWO	45
CHAPTER 5	46
CHAPTER 6	59
CHAPTER 7	70
PART THREE	81
CHAPTER 8	82
CHAPTER 9	97
CHAPTER 10	105

CHAPTER 1

The Marketing Agency That Went From $350,000 in Debt to $1.75 Million in Profit

Simon's day started with the same gut-wrenching feeling that he had felt for some time. He didn't get much sleep last night, so he wasn't eager to get out of bed when morning came.

Still, the day had to start somewhere, and for Simon, that meant doing the morning routine he'd developed over the past weeks. It didn't involve exercise, breakfast, or a coffee ritual. Instead, Simon logged into his bank account.

Checking his bank balance was futile; Simon knew he'd see the same numbers but nervously felt the urge to do it anyway.

"Yep," he thought, *"no change from yesterday."*

Simon was over $300,000 in the negative.

He logged off, and the same thoughts started running through his mind. Would today be the day when he got that dreaded call from the bank, finally pulling the plug? What if he just turned his phone off, crossed his fingers, and hoped for the best?

Maybe a miracle would happen, and things would somehow change by tomorrow.

Simon knew that was unlikely.

The depressing routine went as it always did, with Simon taking a nervous pace around the room, sitting down, and realizing he had no clue what he was going to do.

Back when Simon started his marketing agency, he had no reason to expect things would go so wrong. The company was initially a success, not only for itself but also for its clients. Simon helped so many people build a brand and amass a fortune, and his agency trained and created careers for hundreds, if not thousands.

It seemed like the sky was the limit.

Yet, while his clients and employees ended up making millions, buying cars and houses he could only dream of, Simon's business peaked, then started to decline.

As the debt kept growing, Simon found himself overwhelmed, frantically trying to keep up. He started working insane hours and borrowed against his retirement accounts. He had put everything he had into the business and still didn't have anything to show for it.

In fact, Simon was spending so much time at work that he hardly got to see his two kids. Even worse, he and his family were on the brink of losing their home.

No one could expect anything less than a complete disaster from a situation like this. However, that's not what happened to Simon.

Despite his horrible predicament, Simon is living his dream life today. His agency is profitable again, and he's working less than eight hours a week.

You might wonder what could have possibly happened to produce such a 180° turn in Simon's life; he found the help he so desperately needed. Of course, the full story is more complex, and we'll explain it in detail in the following sections.

Where Was the Agency Before?

At one point, Simon's agency was making a decent amount of money. It had 35 employees and some big clients. The company followed the hourly billing model and was making the industry average of $72 average hourly earnings.

So, how did a marketing agency like that end up with only a handful of employees, more than $300,000 in debt, a negative bank balance, and an owner fruitlessly putting everything into the business?

The answer is in the underlying issues that made it seem like Simon's company was doing okay. The financial struggle was constant, and the company's time and resources were stretched thin at all times.

The company had anchored itself to one major client. When that client went away, Simon's business collapsed, almost to the point of no return.

However, one thing in particular caused the company to crumble: the lack of specialization.

Simon's company did everything across the board. Whatever the client could imagine, they got. Digital advertising, traditional media buying, experiential, conventions, demos, events, websites, landing pages, email marketing. You name it – everything was on the table.

The company would do anything for anybody with utter disregard for the internal cost.

Imagine going to a Porsche dealership and saying something like this: *"I want your car, but I want you to remove the roof, add custom spoilers, replace the engine, and throw in some leopard pattern seat covers."*

That's how Simon's clients approached his company. Of course, it turned out that the generalist model was highly inefficient, which is precisely why you can't demand carte blanche customization when, say, buying a Porsche.

This issue had a severe impact on Simon's business. It lost a lot of revenue and almost went bankrupt. Luckily, Simon found the help they needed before everything fell apart completely.

The Recovery Process

The state Simon's company was in when we, Creative Agency Success, started working with them was past dire.

Often, a business can get through a situation akin to a small fire in the corridor. Someone just needs to go and put it out, and everything can return to normal.

In Simon's case, it was more akin to people smoking in a fireworks factory.

Calls about payments were coming in every day, and the only thing Simon could do was apologize. After a while, each workday ended in him leaving the office in tears.

We had to completely overhaul the most significant components of the business to begin the recovery. However, once that process was complete, the results were astonishing.

The method we used to remove the issues Simon's business suffered from relied on three key overhauls: sales and lead generation, operations, and pricing. By changing these three aspects, we helped Simon's company to course-correct and become truly profitable.

The Sales and Lead Generation Overhaul

In terms of sales and lead generation, one crucial change had to happen to create a foundation for the overhaul. Simon's company had to specialize and position itself as an authority in the market.

One of their biggest claims to fame was in consumer-packaged goods, food and beverage, with an emphasis on the Hispanic market. This was the specialization that we decided to lean on completely.

Once the company doubled down on that part of the market, we shifted the focus to specific services, namely experiential and events. Aside from some rare exceptions, the business reformed around these services entirely.

The specialization allowed us to formulate the company's offer much more precisely, and it was time to work on positioning and establishing a presence in the market.

Simon's agency had been in the industry for a long time, which, in theory, gave it potential for working with large brands. The necessary contacts were certainly there, but so were the issues that resulted from the company's downfall.

The business couldn't get through risk review at large brands to become an approved vendor for the multi-million contracts it wanted. Risk review is used to understand what percentage of the agency's revenue goes into annual spending on the contract. If that number is higher than 30%, it raises a red flag because it's considered that the agency could destabilize and create significant issues for the brand.

We recommended a different approach. Simon's company would create regional tours with brands where each brand would only pay for a portion of the tour.

This model resolved the risk problem, and, at that point, everything was ready for a new marketing strategy to be put in place.

Marketing for Simon's company had to start with great outreach. We decided that LinkedIn would be the ideal place because it was a massive network with an abundance of potential leads and information about other businesses. After all, Simon had already built a considerable list of contacts in the industry. This meant he could achieve high impact with relatively little effort.

With a clearly defined offer in place, there were no obstacles to reaching out to their ideal client. We knew it wouldn't take long before prospects started coming in, and it became essential to define one more aspect of sales and lead generation: the sales process.

The tactic we employed relied on universal and repeatable principles. The vital principle is to offer one primary type of service and deliver it in a specific way, which we'd already achieved with Simon's company.

Sales and delivery are interlinked to a high degree. When there's a stable, repeatable delivery process in place, it's much easier to position the offer so that it converts.

Since we've achieved all of those goals with the sales and lead generation overhaul, Simon's company was ready to get out on the market. However, this wasn't the only change we introduced.

The Operational Overhaul

If there's one aspect of running a company that most creatives avoid, it's operations. While far removed from the glitz and glamour of business, it's still an essential component in ensuring a company's success.

Luckily, Simon understood that overhauling his company's operations was the crucial step on the road to recovery. This allowed us to improve the business using two critical methods: time studies and defined operational processes.

Time studies are an essential tool in determining operational blocks. Most of the time, there's a specific block in the funnel, which can be a single person who everybody needs to go through.

This issue can be resolved by coming up with a way to disperse the communication between multiple people effectively. Once the block is removed, the company can have a free flow of information. For Simon's agency, it was him. Fortunately, this also meant that he would be removed from being the central person in his agency, providing much-needed and desired relief.

Standard Operating Procedures or SOPs present a solution for another operational problem that occurs very often. When a company has been in business for a long time, people often over-engineer processes around every single issue that arises. Once these processes amass, they can start clogging up the overall operations.

As a company that initially had 35 employees and a lot of problems, Simon's business was naturally prone to this pitfall.

To counteract this negative phenomenon, we deconstructed the entire operations and laid out the processes in a comprehensible fashion.

The method we used to do this involved writing down every task that went into deliverables, from contract signing to project closing. Then, we put the tasks in the order in which they should happen and assigned them to different roles. Finally, we created a project checklist based on the ordered tasks.

This universal method for better operational organization helped Simon's company become efficient and establish reliable processes. Now that the market approach and deliverables were improved, there was one more thing to do: overhaul the pricing model.

The Pricing Overhaul

Before working with us, Simon's company used a variable, cost-plus pricing model. This caused a range of issues, including the company's services being underpriced, which, in turn, led to the business becoming unprofitable.

Our solution to the pricing problem was to pivot towards fixed value-based pricing, and it was the right choice.

The typical gross profit margin in the experiential event planning industry is between 25% and 40%. Once the pricing model was changed, Simon's company hit a gross profit of 68%, previously unheard of within that industry.

The crucial advantage of fixed pricing was that it represented a scalable and accurate model. However, it was necessary to set the model up so that nothing was missed. We had to go through various formats before structuring the pricing in a way that ensured maximum profitability.

Fixed value-based pricing allowed Simon's company to start charging premium prices and move away from a faulty model that caused them severe problems. With that final overhaul in place, the business was ready to get back on its feet.

Simon's Agency Transformed

With our guidance, Simon's company managed to improve its lead generation, sales process, operations, and pricing model. The impact these changes made reflected on everything, from team and customer satisfaction to financial metrics.

Finally, the recovered business had all the resources it needed to deliver its services seamlessly. More and more clients started coming in, but the company's team was no longer overworked because they had plenty of time to focus on the important things, providing value to clients.

After the specialization, the company could devote full attention to the clients' needs. This led to everyone feeling happy about the business. The team was satisfied because they could achieve the expected results with less effort, the clients were overjoyed with the quality of the deliverables, and Simon could hardly believe the transformation.

The business became profitable beyond expectations, and this was in large part due to the implemented changes that allowed the company's values to shine.

From a debt of over $300,000, the business grew to seven, and then eight figures. It was making an average hourly earnings of almost $500, over a five-fold increase. Revenue also jumped up about nine times.

Finally, the day came when Simon was no longer waking up feeling uneasy. Instead of trembling before his account balance, he could now look at the numbers with pride and joy.

The dreaded debt was no longer present, and Simon's company made a profit of $1.75 million.

Simon regained freedom, both for himself and his business. Financially, things were going great, but, more importantly, Simon had the time to devote to his family. He was finally free of the overwhelming stress and tiredness.

These impressive results were made possible because of particular approaches that we took. This approach differed from others because it didn't adhere to conventional practices, demonstrating that creative solutions can be the best course of action in many cases.

Moving Away From Conventional Wisdom

Conventional wisdom in business refers to the view of how things should be run generally. However, following this philosophy ensures mediocrity and is not how we at Creative Agency Success define great business. Profit, Impact, and Freedom is what success means to us; it's everything that provides the business owner with the life they truly desire.

Of course, we understand best practices and their merits. But we also recognize that businesses need to allow their demographics to guide their final decisions and the nuances behind them.

Doing things by a common template can get you up to a certain point. Some businesses will stay afloat beyond that point, while many others will require more specific methods that fall outside conventional wisdom to thrive. We believe that dogmatically following conventional wisdom is the root cause of why 97% of agencies never reach seven figures.

Imagine two digital advertising agencies. One sells to lawyers, while the other works with hair salons. Conventional wisdom would suggest that both agencies could employ the same model and be successful.

However, when you consider the pricing, business challenges, offers, and ways of communicating with these specific types of clients, it becomes obvious that these two agencies will need different strategies. After all, they're working with entirely different clients, with different psychographic personas.

The way that we're moving away from conventional wisdom is through understanding such nuances and devising the necessary adjustments to account for them.

In the case of Simon's company, this approach helped the agency achieve a dramatic turnaround. And that leads us to the aim of this book.

What you're about to read in the following chapters is intended for creative agencies that want help in making those necessary adjustments to reach a seven-figure or greater annual revenue.

If your agency fits that profile, feel free to continue reading. And if you're

eager to get started right away, you can do that by reaching out at
creativeagencysuccess.com/startnow

CHAPTER 2

Who This Book Is (and Isn't) For

It would be best to clarify one thing before moving forward:

If your agency is already well-established and you're only looking for methods for scaling or succession planning, this book won't be for you.

However, it will be of interest to agency owners who still do client work and struggle to grow consistently. If you feel like a hamster on a wheel and want to break free, you're the ideal audience for this book.

There's a glass ceiling when it comes to typical agency development, and it's $1 million. Most agencies stay below that number – 97% of them, to be precise. Breaking that glass ceiling and sharing actionable advice on how to become a seven-plus-figure business is the very subject we'll be covering here.

Agency owners who've already broken into the 3% will gain more from our other book (*The Agency Blueprint*) that's geared towards that specific demographic.

If you belong to the group of agency owners who are looking for ways to take their business to the next level, you'll probably want to know another thing:

What makes the authors of this book competent to give such crucial advice?

This is the ideal opportunity to introduce ourselves. We're Robert Patin and Darren D. Ward from Creative Agency Success. You're about to read our stories, from our early days to becoming experts in creative agency business improvement.

Robert's Story

One of the most impactful moments from my childhood memories has to do with a pair of shoes.

When I was a kid, my mom struggled for money. I remember that she had these old, worn, tattered shoes where you could actually see her foot through the bottom. That's what she wore to work every day.

At the same time, I saw kids at school whose parents were better off financially. Like any other kid in that situation, I wanted something that would make me fit in with that crowd. Growing up poor was hard enough without being singled out in school.

I developed an obsession with a particular model of Jordans that I'd seen some kids wearing. It was more of a symbolic than practical thing. I knew that I'd probably never have those shoes, and it made me profoundly sad.

Imagine my surprise when mom showed up one day with those very same Jordans! Almost two years have passed since I first told her that I wanted the shoes, and she spent most of that period saving up money to buy them.

Not only that – she actually drove many hours out of her way to find them.

At first, it took some convincing to make me even take them out of the box. All I wanted to do was keep those shoes in there, perfect as I've always imagined them. But once I finally took them out, I was ecstatic and couldn't wait to take my new shoes to school. I was burning with pride and the desire to show them to everyone.

That was the first time I realized that, when something really matters to you and you're ready to do whatever it takes to manifest it into reality, it becomes possible. The fact that my mom saved money and bought me those shoes made me feel happy and accepted. The sheer force of will had made something so seemingly unlikely happen. It was a more valuable experience than any number could express, and it taught me that every circumstance can change. I understood that, rather than accepting the things I don't like, I could take action and change them.

The next crucial lesson I got was when my parents sent me to a private school.

I was fully aware of the sacrifices they both had to make to achieve that. They worked extremely hard and spent next to nothing on themselves to ensure a better future for me.

Knowing what it took my parents to send me to the private school and being surrounded by privileged kids made me tenacious. I started striving to accomplish something to justify everything that my parents invested in me.

Luckily, I had some traits that helped me along the way. As a precocious problem solver, I was always able to spot the closest route to eventual success and find solutions to various problems. In fact, that's the very thing I do today.

However, I didn't find my ideal profession straight away.

In my early 20s, I spent a lot of time seeking a creative career in art and photography. While I eventually realized that wasn't the right path for me, the experiences from that period made me highly effective at working alongside creatives.

The best career choice for me turned out to be related to the qualities I had naturally.

I understood that I was an analytical problem solver, not a creative one. I was never going to be a new Jackson Pollock, but I could help the Pollocks of the world to achieve success with their talents.

A deep understanding and appreciation of the mindset and processes of creatives enabled me to help numerous creative agencies accomplish their goals. At the same time, the way I grew up and was educated taught me much about wealth. I was able to see what affluence meant, how it could benefit people, and, most importantly, how to achieve it.

Once all of the pieces of the puzzle fell into place, I decided that I wanted to start working with agencies to sort out their problems. This turned out to be the winning combination for me, as well as for those creative agencies I've helped. I spent a significant period working internally at agencies on a full-time basis.

One experience after another, I started to discern precisely what worked and what didn't. As a result of that practice, I've managed to take numerous agencies to a point where they've grown their revenue and profits by several times. This experience and the unique combination of my natural traits, insights, and education made me an expert in the field.

During my career, I've learned some crucial things about myself and the value that I can provide to clients.

First, my childhood struggles, and especially the struggles of my parents, made me the person I am today. They gave me the passion for reaching higher and seeking out creative solutions to challenges.

Second, I realized the importance of customized solutions. I know that there isn't one thing that I could say to everyone to produce the same results across the board. The same goes for this book – it isn't a silver bullet. Instead, it's a reliable outline for a method that can help you achieve success.

Finally, I learned that I'm not "smarter" than the people I help. When I start advising an agency, the only advantage I've got compared to the creatives I'm working with is that I've been through the process before.

Whatever the problem may be and whatever solution we're looking for, chances are that I've done those things before and now understand precisely how to apply them.

Darren's Story

My name is Darren Ward, and I come from the second most boring place to live in California – Lancaster.

When my family moved to Lancaster, they welcomed the boredom with a sense of relief. It's because the inner city LA culture was not an ideal environment for young kids to grow up in. The city was overwhelmed with gang culture, the crack epidemic raging. And one day, when my family was at home, there was a loud bang outside. Everyone knew that it was a gunshot – they've become familiar with the sound, although they'd never heard it so close to home before.

My mother went to the window to check what was going on, saw something, and opened the door. Right on our porch was a dead body. Someone got killed on our very doorstep. My family started to pack the next day.

Now, growing up in Lancaster clearly had its benefits, but it didn't take long for me to realize that the place didn't sit well with my temperament.

I have always been a high-energy kid. I could never sit still – I had to be doing something all the time. Combined with an insatiable curiosity, this made me a real handful and turned out to be very risky in certain situations.

One time, our family car got overheated on the freeway, and we were towed to the mechanic shop. When we arrived, my dad went to the front of the car and was checking under the hood with the mechanic.

Curious to see what they were doing, I started to harass my mom to let me out. At the fifteenth time of asking, she gave in and allowed me to go. I dashed out of the car and got near the hood. Instead of paying attention to what was going on, I got distracted by a glassy mirror door they had at the shop.

All of a sudden, I saw everybody running away from the car in that glass mirror, and I swung around. In a fraction of a second, the radiator fluid exploded all over me, burning over three-quarters of my body. As a result, I had to spend an entire year in bandages, all due to a simple lack of attention during one fateful moment.

As strange as it may seem, this played a massive role in my life and, eventually, my career.

Whenever I see a client who rushes in a particular direction without a clear focus, I instinctively bristle. I also remember how long it took me to recover from something that happened in a blink of an eye, and, time and again, experience has shown me that in business as in life, everything can change when you least expect it.

Getting burned in business can be every bit as bad as getting burned by radiator fluid. And I've decided to always do my best to prevent that from happening.

I want to share an example of just that kind of situation.

I had a client during the coronavirus pandemic who was about to lose some 70% of their revenue. The client called me and said that we needed to start putting together a layoff plan.

That's when the childhood memory kicked in, and I had a knee-jerk response. Chaos was ensuing, and everything was starting to burn. Yet, instead of trying to put the fire out, this client was panicking and about to add grease to it.

I responded by telling them to s l o w d o w n.

We started talking, trying to carefully figure out what the issues were, and I explained that there might be a potential opportunity in all of it.

Luckily, the client listened to my advice and ended up changing their strategy and retargeting rather than downsizing. Within two months, they managed to recoup almost all of the revenue they'd lost.

Of course, there was much more that formed me into the person I am today than that accident. A pivotal moment in early adulthood happened when I transitioned to college. The newfound freedom was overwhelming and quickly bored me. With more time on my hands than I knew what to do with, I ended up staying in my dorm room all of the time. Complaining about this to my father, he turned around and gave me a piece of lifechanging advice.

He told me to make my life what I wanted it to be. In fact, he challenged me to create the life that I imagined, that I had the opportunity in front of me and wasn't doing anything with it when I could've done anything.

My competitive spirit kicked in, and I took the challenge to heart. I revived a college club, traveled to Japan as a U.S. Ambassador for student relations, and even spoke on a panel for the White House.

By the time I was about to graduate, the president of my school was so impressed that he wrote a letter of recommendation to the University of Miami. As a result, I got into the Accelerated Business program, forging my lifelong pursuit of knowledge in analytics and negotiations.

We can always create the opportunity we want, and that's as true in business as it is in life. If you have the momentum, commitment, and motivation, you can do anything.

When you harness where you are and what you have and adapt to it, you can move forward and accomplish your goals.

Our Goal Is to Help You Succeed Faster

Now that you know who we are, it's time to learn more about how we help people build their businesses to success.

We sometimes compare what we do to the job of an audio engineer. A band recording an album has all of the creativity and ideas, but that doesn't always guarantee that the record will sell.

An expert needs to come in and transform the sounds into something that will hit the market in the way the band wants. Without that crucial component, even the best piece of music could end up never reaching the listeners.

This analogy applies very well to what we do at Creative Agency Success. We focus on working with creative agencies and helping them to grow their business. While we understand the processes and the energy behind the agency, we're not there as creatives in the same sense of the word.

Instead, we help agencies harness that energy and turn it into something truly amazing and profitable. And through our vast experience in this industry, the methods we use to that end are proven and reliable.

In this book, we'll explain what happens behind the scenes when Creative Agency Success starts working with a client. The three main sections will outline each crucial element of the process:

1. Attracting clients
2. Converting prospects into paying clients
3. Delivering amazing results

Once you reach the final pages, we're certain you'll have a much deeper understanding of the vital steps necessary to achieve your agency's goals.

Are you interested in connecting with other agency owners like yourself – while learning leading industry tactics on a weekly basis?

We have a dedicated group for creative agency owners. Each member gains access to proven and implementable systems that will help them to:

- Get a consistent stream of new leads each month
- Convert leads into new clients without a long sales process
- Deliver a quality service that works with less involvement from you

You can join for free right now via www.creativeagencysuccess.com/join

PART ONE

Attracting Clients

CHAPTER 3

Specialization and the Desirable Offer

Everybody knows how Apple revolutionized the computer industry. Since its inception in 1976, the company has spearheaded innovation in the field and become synonymous with technological progress.

Apple's founders, Steve Wozniak and Steve Jobs, have likewise become universally recognized figures celebrated as geniuses. However, the two visionaries and their company would've never achieved the success they have were it not for a crucial move that Jobs made.

In the beginning, the vision for Apple was based on the first product that Steve Wozniak created. It was supposed to be a board that would serve as the basis for people to build their computers.

This would've been very similar to a PC in the sense that there would be a platform for custom-built computers with parts from various manufacturers. But Steve Jobs had a different idea.

Although Jobs wasn't a computer technician, he had a clear vision of what Apple should become. He wanted to create a specialized, fully enclosed computer that would have everything from the operating system and the chips inside to the keyboard made by Apple. In Jobs' vision, the computer would be completely designed and curated for the consumer.

This philosophy of an enclosed and specialized niche product inspired all of the breakthrough devices that earned Apple its name, from the original Macintosh computer to the iPhone.

To this day, Apple produces its own hardware and software, as well as design solutions. Owing to Steve Jobs' vision, Apple is a recognizable brand that stands for both functionality and luxury.

Undoubtedly, specialization made Apple the giant that it is today. It allowed the company to offer high-ticket products, provide great value, and become one of the most profitable businesses in the world.

At the same time, the company's success is a testament to the importance of specializing and niching. Apple was never interested in pursuing customers outside of its niche. Instead, the company focused on the people who would find its products the most appealing and doubled down on creating the perfect product for them.

Now, millions of people use Apple products, but that's not because the company decided to abandon the idea of specialization. Rather, the brand that they've established has become so respected that it drew more people into Apple's niche.

Niching is a crucial element of business. Even if it seems that you'd be better off as a jack of all trades, the opposite is true. As proven by Apple and many other successful companies, finding a specialization and carving a clear path in one well-defined direction is the best way to go.

Why Is Your Niche So Important?

"The only way to do great work is to love what you do." – Steve Jobs

Niching gives your agency focus, and this is something that many organizations fail to realize. Typically, they come from a scarcity mindset and try to get as much business as possible by covering the entire market.

Steve Jobs left Apple for several years. When he came back, the company was in huge trouble because it had abandoned its original vision. While Jobs was absent, Apple started pushing out more and more products and losing focus. This turned out to be a mistake that created a loss of $1 billion.

Once Jobs returned and became CEO, the first thing he did was to cancel 70% of their offerings. Apple quickly focused back on the core products and high-end home computers, their niche from the start.

The company worked hard on those products, making a $300 million gain in the following years. Apple only moved on to promoting new products once it mastered the personal computer market.

The company started by catering to one specific demographic, growing and scaling in what it did best. It didn't begin with the massive offer it has today. Instead, Apple specialized and created a foundation for expanding its services.

Specialization and niching are incredibly beneficial because they remove many struggles businesses and agencies face, especially in the initial phases.

Without a niche, you can find your resources stretched thin. Servicing an entire market requires more than most agencies can handle, and those that attempt it end up hard-pressed for time and money.

Even if you can be a jack of all trades on your own, the real trouble starts when your agency begins to scale. At that point, you might find it very challenging to replace yourself because other people in your team aren't as versatile. At the same time, you're doing so many things at once that creating a functioning process becomes nigh impossible.

In other words, no one else can do the job for you, and you can't establish a system that allows others to be efficient at it.

All of the pressure that builds up in such an environment also doesn't produce good results for clients. Apple excelled at what they did because they didn't try to push out Mac, iPad, and iPhone all at the same time. They perfected one product before moving on to others. By doing so, they were able to provide the best results for their customers.

Maintaining focus on its niche simultaneously allowed Apple to attract more clients. Since the company became excellent at what it did, it earned a great reputation, making people want to become a part of their ecosystem.

This could never happen with a generalist approach. If you don't have a particularly strong point and focus, it's much harder to advertise what you do and attract new people to work with you. However, even this isn't the end of the troubles you face without specialization.

Agencies that aren't seen as experts in their field can have a very hard time charging higher or even profitably sustainable fees for their services. Although you might put in the same amount of work as a specialist, you'll most likely end up providing a low-cost service, and this happens as a result of two factors.

First, as a generalist agency, you usually end up taking any clients you can get. In other words, you don't have the luxury of saying *No*. When you can't choose your clients, it becomes more and more challenging to dictate the price of your work.

After all, people need to see your offer as something special to accept paying a premium price. But without niching, you'll end up sounding just like any other agency out there and will, in turn, be paid as such.

Second, your clients want to know that they're working with an expert who's in control of the situation. That's the only way they'll agree to a high-ticket service. Your clients need to trust you to take them in the right direction, and they can't do that if your agency doesn't have a history of expertise in the field.

To summarize why niching is important, you want to position yourself as someone who's done the work before and provided excellent value to their clients. That's how you can avoid all the common struggles of generalist agencies and establish your presence on the market as someone very good at solving a particular set of problems.

Once you do that, your agency can grow and scale gradually while providing your clients with the best service possible. Niching is the best way to ensure that you're helping your clients and your business at the same time.

However, niching down requires plenty of attention and deliberation. You don't want to start working with just any niche. Instead, you'll want to create a careful selection that will relate to the vision you have for your agency.

How to Select a Niche

When selecting your niche, you should start by answering three crucial questions: what are the characteristics of your niche, who do you want to be in the market, and, most importantly, what is your passion?

On a more detailed level, these questions include vital considerations:

- Do you enjoy the people in your niche?
- Is that industry growing?
- Will the industry be more relevant 10 years from now than it is today?
- Can you help your niche?
- Can the people within the niche afford you?

In terms of qualifying the characteristics of your ideal niche, the matter is relatively straightforward. You'll want to determine the industry you want to work with, the service you can provide to that market, and the geographic area your agency will cover.

The crucial consideration here is that you need to understand what it is that you do best, your "superpower." It's a question of who your clients will be and how qualified you are to resolve their issues – the industry and the service.

A pressing matter that needs to be expanded upon is modern communications and the internet. The impediment of geographical proximity doesn't matter much anymore when specializing.

When you have those basics down, you'll need to decide who you want to be as an agency. This relates to the type of clients and the number of niches that you take on.

Many agencies strive to work with enterprise clients purely because that kind of work seems flashier. However, the truth of the matter is that not every agency can handle such clients, and it can quickly turn out to be less fun than it looks.

A similar thing applies to the number of niches that you decide to work with. Going overboard on that front can be a critical mistake because you can end up stretching your resources thin just as if you were a generalist agency. Ideally, you'll want to cover a single niche or possibly two. In exceptional circumstances, you could even take on a third. But never go above three to avoid overwhelming your agency. In fact, we strongly suggest one niche.

These choices will determine who you are within your niche. Together with the qualifications, they'll help you define your specialization and let your clients know precisely what you do. However, the most important thing is your passion.

Now, many people think that their job is one thing and their passion something else entirely. They spend their workdays doing something that pays the bills and leave the things they're passionate about for the weekends.

This approach is understandable. After all, when you find a job, you can remove all of the stress and stop worrying about your daily expenses. Then, you can live a happy, comfortable life and be relaxed about pursuing your passion in your spare time.

Another point supporting this attitude is that if your passion becomes your job, it might quickly extinguish that flame. Just because you're passionate about something, it doesn't mean you can monetize it. It can become a source of additional stress instead of something that brings you joy.

As much as this argument seems convincing, there are some strong counterpoints to it. First of all, people are rarely that one-sided in life. Your daily job doesn't have to categorize you in such a strict way, nor does your passion need to stay reserved for your free time.

As an agency owner, you likely don't envision yourself as someone who wakes up in the morning thinking, *"Oh God, I don't want to go to work today!"*

You want to make a mark on the world and give what you do greater meaning. And, of course, there will be days when you just want to lay in bed – no one's immune to that feeling. But more often than not, you'll be happy to show up and help people you enjoy working with doing the work that you love.

Another important point is that we shouldn't mistake things that we *enjoy* with what we're passionate about. You might enjoy a million different things, like music, movies, traveling, or various hobbies. But your passion is what drives you forward, and it's the thing that you're good at that energizes you.

When you turn your passion into a job, it won't become a menial nine-tofive thing. It's going to be something you can design your life around and be eager to do every day. Best of all, your clients will pick up on that feeling quickly.

The greatest benefit of selecting a niche based on your passion is that you're able to draw people in. You can speak eloquently and with energy about your job and transfer that flame to your clients. But this is only possible if you're truly passionate about what you do.

Once you've carved out your niche following these crucial aspects, you'll have a specialized agency that's ready to get involved in the market. However, before you start taking on clients, you'll need to create an offer that corresponds with your niche.

Structuring Your Offer

Creating a great offer depends entirely on how well you understand your niche. It is a matter of fact that people buy a service because they have a specific problem that they need solved. In particular, they seek out a service to alleviate pain or provide pleasure.

When you know your audience, you'll also know their biggest pain points. Then, you can tailor your offer to alleviate those pain points and provide your clients with the goals they want to achieve.

On the other side of that equation will be your ability to deliver on that offer and give the client the result they're looking for. If you want to create such an offer, you'll need to understand some core principles.

Don't Try to Be a Jack of All Trades

The specialization you chose is the core of your agency, and your offer should clearly reflect that. While this might sound straightforward, it's a crucial step that many agencies get wrong.

In fact, we've worked with many agencies that were very vague about what they do. If you went on one of their websites, you'd only see that they were a branding or a digital agency, and you'd have no clue about what precisely they did.

This mistake in formulating an offer is probably a remnant of the generalist mindset where people don't want to state what their service is to leave the playing field open. However, if you've chosen to niche down, you'll need to go all-in and present your offer in a specialized manner.

Don't Talk About Yourself

Another thing to avoid is what we call "selling to your competition." This means your offer is presented as if you're targeting people in your industry rather than your clients.

These kinds of offers involve websites that talk about all of the agency's achievements and the phenomenal work it does. The issue here is that your clients simply don't care about that side of your job. They don't want to hear about the great things you've done or the awards that you've won.

Your clients need a solution for *their* problems, and that's what your offer should be all about. It's best to avoid turning it into an ego platform and focus on your prospect's goals and needs.

Show Clients That You're an Advisor Who Can Guide Them

The main reason why your clients come to you is that you're the expert. They're looking for someone who'll be their go-to for any advice and problem solving, and that's how you'll want to present your agency.

Your offer should send the message that you're the service provider, advisor, consultant, and problem solver that your clients need. When they look at your offer, they should know that you can guide them to where they want to go.

Clients in your niche should realize that they need your service and that it's the best option for them. They should see you as a water vendor that they came upon in the middle of a desert. Just as they wouldn't care about anything else but quenching their thirst in that situation, your clients should jump at the opportunity for you to resolve their issues.

How to Write an Offer

The most important aspect of your offer is that it's understandable. When you start writing your offer, it should explain to your clients what you're actually offering, how you'll deliver on that offer, and what results they'll get.

To achieve that level of clarity, naturally, you'll need to understand those points yourself. That's the crucial thing you'll get from specialization and niching. Then, you should also make sure that you're using the language of your clients and their persona.

This consideration is important because there are many jargons for various issues, and the language you use every day might not be as comprehensible for your clients. That's why it's not only about *what* you say in your offer but *how* you phrase it.

The KISS (Keep It Simple Stupid) Principle

The best way to think about your offer is as something you could explain in a sentence or two to a friend at a barbecue. Imagine that your friend doesn't know anything about advertising, technology, or any other aspect of your work, and you need to help them understand what you do with a single sentence.

This is the KISS principle, and it's the basis of the best marketing out there.

The point of this principle is that you should create an offer using simple language that anyone can understand. However, it goes a bit beyond mere understanding.

When your clients read your offer, they should say, *"Oh, that's me! You're talking about my goals, frustrations, desires, and the things I'm struggling with. You're talking about me."*

Road Testing the Offer

People buy a service from a purely emotional place. That's why your offer should be more about speaking to the emotion than about trying to be a tactical, smart wordsmith. It's a matter of talking to the person you're trying to help and showing your own humanity.

The vital aspect of the emotional approach to offering your services is that its effectiveness isn't immediately apparent. If you don't test your offer, you won't know whether or not it resonates.

If you want to make sure that your offer gets to your clients and can convert their opinion, you'll need to do some analysis and research. This is where your demo will become critical. Ideally, you should understand how your clients feel and what they think when they hear your offer.

Building a Model Around Your Offer

Once you create an ideal offer for your niche that resonates, you should start orientating your agency to align with that offer. In this case, your creativity will be key, and, as an agency owner, you already have a creative aspect as a part of your motivation for starting the agency in the first place.

When you get to building a model of services for your niche, you'll have to factor in not only your clients but also the way your agency will work. Of course, you want to move forward in a creative, inspired way and do fun things within your niche. But you'll also want to think about another crucial piece of the puzzle: your client's revenue.

The model we prefer is based on monthly recurring revenue, which ensures that all the bills are paid, the company's profitable, and everything is nice and secure, freeing you to put your undivided focus into the work. If you build this model around your offer, you'll be able to put both your clients and your agency in a place where you receive plenty of revenue each month.

When you manage to do that, you'll remove any stress or anxiety about upcoming projects and, with some course correction along the way, design a model that will always provide results for your clients. All this will become possible once you specialize and choose your niche.

Gift #1 - Specialization Download

By now, it should be clear that niching down and specializing provides massive benefits for your agency.

Knowing the difference between being a niched agency vs. a full-service agency is more important than ever.

And to put the theory into successful practice, you need to know the following:

- How the three billing models (hourly rate, fixed fee, and retainer) perform in the real world.
- Best practices of the top 100 creative agencies in the country.
- The specific challenges that creative agencies face at different stages of growth.

All that (and more) is covered in our free interactive industry report. Download it here: creativeagencysuccess.com/resources

CHAPTER 4

Prospecting

Imagine a woman in a red dress walking into a room full of people. She doesn't say a thing, yet the entire room falls silent. Everyone's jaw drops to the floor, and they don't even know what's happened.

It's not that the woman's just breathtaking and desirable. No, she has a certain aura about her that exudes elegance. With one look, people understand that she's as knowledgeable and intelligent as she is welldressed.

This scene isn't purely imaginary – there are people in the world who have such a level of charisma that everyone wants to be near them. In fact, certain brands and agencies have it, too.

Think about Brioni or Ferrari. Those brands don't have to convince people to buy their tailor-made suits or customized cars. They are so attractive that people feel drawn to them on their own. Such brands are the business equivalent of the woman in the red dress, and they have a trait that your agency should strive for: they're irresistible.

Why is it important to become irresistible to your clients? Because you don't have to go up to people and sell yourself to them. Instead, they'll come to you, and your entire sales process will become much easier.

This is a crucial point when it comes to selling, especially because so many agencies have a problem with the concept of sales. Faced with the possibility of rejection, people tend to get overly eager and too forward. At that point, their prospects receive all of the power, and the offer at hand becomes less desirable.

Think back to the stunning woman in the red dress. With all of her elegance, intelligence, and charisma, she would undoubtedly take command of a conversation should anyone approach her. And that's in part because everybody else would be awestruck in her presence.

As strange as it sounds, the same principle applies to selling your services. If you approach your clients with an overblown desire to sell, you'll be that awestruck person who automatically relinquishes command of the conversation.

What you want to become in your sales process is, metaphorically, the woman in the red dress. You want to be comfortable about it and create an atmosphere where your clients are eager to work with you, not the other way around.

In this chapter, we'll show you how to build up your outbound sales and inbound marketing to achieve just that.

Outbound Sales Is Needed (So Get Over It)

"If you can't advertise yourself, what hope have you being able to advertise anything else."

– David Ogilvy

Certain stereotypical images come to mind regarding sales. For example, one of them might be a sleazy car salesperson. You likely know or have experienced this stereotype – it's the person who tries to sell you that secondhand convertible by any means necessary, convincing you that it's actually a good thing that the roof doesn't go all the way up or that the crack on the windshield is just an easy fix.

This is the type of salesperson that people talk about outsmarting when they manage to get a bargain. Their sales technique is based on a desperate need to sell and a complete disregard of their value.

Well, you certainly didn't start an agency to become a used car salesperson.

What you want to be is an Aston Martin dealer. Someone who sells a classy, elegant product that will make your clients fall in love with it.

Contrary to what some might think, you can achieve just that through outbound sales. In fact, if you don't have an expertly made, defined lead generation engine, you'll find that outbound is necessary. When you approach it with the mindset of selling a desirable premium product, the process will become more comfortable, and you'll be able to present your offer with clarity and grace.

Why Outbound Has a Place in Modern Marketing

Outbound sales is relevant in the modern market for the same reason as always. People don't know who you are, what you do, or what purpose your agency serves if you're not actively marketing your agency. That's where outbound sales come in as a great way to get in front of your potential clients and let them know about your agency.

But as much as outbound is necessary, some people still take issue with this type of sales due to a particular fear that comes with it. People feel like they're interrupting somebody with their calls, and it's easy to start seeing yourself as that used car salesperson from the beginning of this chapter.

However, that's not the case at all. You aren't trying to scam other people into buying a bad product just to get your part of the commissions. In fact, you aren't really selling at all.

What you're actually doing with outbound is – being in service. You're there to help people from your niche who need it, and you want to make them aware of the value you can bring. That's a critical distinction that you must make regarding outbound.

You aren't a salesperson but a service provider and someone who's looking to help clients rather than sell to them.

You Need Outbound

Hopefully, we've dispelled the misconception that outbound is nothing more than picking up the phone and harassing people. Rather, it's a universally useful method of reaching clients and presenting your service. However, there's even more to outbound than that.

Outbound is a scalable way of generating leads, and that's an aspect that many agencies tend to disregard. In fact, most of them simply put out a website, rely on organic marketing, and hope for the best, thinking that people will start coming in any day now. Of course, things don't work that way, and agencies that get this part wrong usually stagnate or have minimal growth.

If you want to grow and scale your agency dependably, you should adopt a different mindset towards outbound and realize that it's more than cold calls and the typical way most agencies go about it. If you do it right, outbound can become a reliable tool that will help your agency reach out to a greater audience and allow you to provide more value in the market. But first, you need to have a thorough understanding of that market, your audience, and the value you'll be bringing into the equation.

Knowing Your Market, Value, and Audience

Whether you're introducing an outbound component through email, social media, or calls, it will need to be targeted and value-driven. It can't be stressed enough how important it is to focus on your value and understand it.

To establish value as the foundation of your marketing and sales, you'll need to get to know your market inside out. That market is your niche and the audience you're addressing, and you'll need to talk to them in words that they'll understand. Communicating your value in a comprehensible way should be your primary task.

When you understand how to talk to your market, you'll find that cold outreach doesn't have to be actually cold. You can invoke emotion and phrase your offer in a more personal way so that it really resonates with your audience. However, the only way you'll be able to do that is if you learn all about what people in your niche are going through and where they need your help.

We discussed this in the previous section when we told you that outbound is more than what agencies usually think. In fact, if you want to do it well, you'll need to devote some attention to the process.

Outbound the Right Way

As mentioned, when you niche down, you study your audience and learn what they're going through. This knowledge can then allow you to write a copy that will speak directly to the people in your target market.

You can address current struggles in the industry and offer your solutions to specific problems in a way that people will immediately resonate with. That's the greatest secret of doing outbound properly. Using the right language, asking the right questions, and addressing relevant issues will show your clients that you're an expert who wants to solve their problems, which will make your outreach compelling.

You can also use outbound to gather more information on your market. Just making a call and presenting your services could be enough to learn whether people are looking for the kind of help you can provide or something else. This can help you tailor your message, improve, and plot a better course for your agency.

When it comes to specific outreach methods, keep in mind that your outbound campaign doesn't have to be massive. In fact, instead of sending out tens of thousands of emails, you can create short videos with small nuggets of advice. Then, you can send those videos to people to give them some value and actionable tips.

The most important part of doing outbound the right way will have to do with how you present yourself. And in this aspect, the universal truth is that you should always be yourself. Don't try to be someone you're not.

This advice sounds like a general remark, but the fact is that we've seen so many people presenting themselves as an expert, saying they can do something they can't, or trying to be a different person.

This approach to sales is both unsuccessful and unnecessary. It's not successful because your prospects will immediately recognize that you aren't genuine. Simultaneously, you'll feel terrible doing it.

It's also unnecessary because you'll always be better off if you're proud of who you are. Talk like you talk, do what you do best, and present yourself naturally. That approach will be much more fruitful in every case.

If you craft compelling copy, focus on solving the market's problems, and act like yourself, you'll have an excellent foundation for doing outbound. Once you set up that process, you can further enhance it with a different, more long-term form of prospecting: inbound marketing.

What About Inbound Marketing?

Inbound marketing is a strategy that takes time and involves building authority, creating relationships, and fine-tuning your lead generation system.

To illustrate how inbound marketing works, you could imagine it as a water pipe with a large number of valves. Some valves might be on, and others might be off, but you don't know which are which, or how far you'd need to turn the valves to maximize the flow.

If there's a blockage somewhere along that water pipe, you'll need to discover where it is, and the best way to do that is to start with the top valve and work your way down. Checking each valve individually will eventually let you know where the problem is. Alternatively, if all valves turn out to be working well, you might need to tap that pipe into a larger water reservoir.

This analogy applies to inbound marketing perfectly. Instead of water in the pipe, you'll be looking at the lead flow and conversion rates in marketing. And through testing different parts of the funnel, you'll be able to determine if there are some choke points along the way.

Like with using water pipe valves, you can also tune your lead funnel through different points. If it turns out that the supply of leads is simply too low, you can tap into another resource.

Once you establish a good flow of leads through your funnel, you can leverage the real power behind inbound marketing. However, to get there, you'll need to understand why inbound marketing matters and how it affects your agency.

What Inbound Marketing Is and How It Helps You Build Authority

If outbound represents anything involving direct outreach, like emails or phone calls, inbound is the opposite. Inbound marketing refers to your website, social media, and the production of any content you make public. It's the form of marketing where people come to your platform to hear your message instead of you reaching out to them.

Inbound marketing can be extremely effective, but only once you build it up. Your greatest responsibility will be to create enough content that people can visit constantly, but this will also be one of the largest benefits.

If you have podcasts, YouTube channels, blog posts, and other content, your audience will be able to look at both your recent and older material, possibly even things you put out years ago. Eventually, you might even get a call from a new client who already knows everything about you.

This opportunity can be precious for your agency because your content can prime potential prospects to convert, because they understand where you're coming from and what you do. The content can nurture your audience without you having to spend as much time with them as you otherwise would.

In other words, inbound marketing can help you build authority in all of the vital aspects. The critical components of authority include connecting with your niche, establishing trust, being likable and knowledgeable, and, finally, speaking in the language of your audience.

With enough inbound marketing content, you'll be able to improve on all of those aspects and, as a result, build a strong authority within your niche.

And if you want to achieve all that, you'll need to choose your content carefully.

Your Website Shouldn't Be Just Your Portfolio

In too many cases, agencies fill out their website with each and every example of their work, as if the only purpose of the website is to showcase how good they are at what they do.

Of course, this is the wrong approach. While the quality of your work is undoubtedly important, it's not what your clients are interested in the most. It's also not why your website exists.

Your website is the central hub of your marketing, and as such, it should work as a 24/7 sales machine and a lead generation engine. You can only enable your website to do that job through appropriate content.

Every piece of content should be directed towards a particular stage of your funnel, from awareness through consideration to decision. Whenever you publish content, you should think about the person who'll be watching it and where they are in the funnel.

Ultimately, your website needs to push your prospects further into the funnel, warm them up, and prime them until they're ready to purchase your services.

Sales Enablement

When it comes to priming your prospect to purchase, the element of sales enablement plays an essential role.

Sales enablement is a function of your sales collateral, such as emails, capabilities decks, and your website and the content that you publish on it. The content in question is success stories, case studies, and testimonials that tell your audience about the results you've achieved.

The goal of these stories is to enable sales on your website and help visitors understand that it would be riskier for them *not* to engage with your services than to engage. But you can only achieve this effect if you stick to the point we've mentioned before:

Don't present success stories and case studies to showcase your work. Use them to showcase the *results*. Show them measurable improvements that resulted from your processes, not the processes themselves. People want to know what challenges your previous clients faced and what you did to resolve them. Keeping this in mind, all of the content you put out there should matter to your audience.

With sales enablement, all other elements of inbound marketing come together, and some new ones get added to the mix. For example, you should pay close attention to an aspect of your website called visitor attention hierarchy.

Visitor attention hierarchy refers to how various elements are ordered on the page. When designing your page, you should work out where you want the visitors to look first, second, third, and fourth. Ensuring what is not there is just as important; slow-load time, confusing navigation, and other seemingly trivial frustrations that act as a drag on-site engagement.

This aspect might sound minor, but it's one of the essential parts that enable your website to sell most efficiently. Make sure that every page element is in the optimal place, and you'll notice the difference in sales.

Content and Becoming Your Own Client

Your content needs to be optimized not only on your website but in every other place on the internet where it appears. With an audience made up largely of internet natives, the first thing you can expect from people is to look you up online when they hear about you.

When that happens, you'll want your prospects to see all of your blog posts, podcasts, and YouTube videos. Furthermore, this shouldn't be limited to your own site but hosted on other websites, too. That's why you should build a network of people to connect with and share your content on their platforms.

Ultimately, your content fulfills another role, which is targeted brand building. This is yet another reason why you'll need to devote plenty of time and energy to planning out that content.

Besides determining what kinds of content you want to publish, you should work out the amount of time that you'll put into working on your content and the frequency at which you'll be publishing it.

It would be best to think in terms of utilizing all of the potentials of your content. Think about how you could repurpose it in different places and channels so that you can maximize the benefits and reduce the time you spend on the entire process.

Finally, become your own client. You don't want to be the shoemaker whose kids don't have shoes. Think about your agency as your dearest client and consider all of the ways in which you could help it grow. If you own a marketing agency, why wouldn't you have a marketing strategy for it?

Gift #2 - Profitability Accelerator Call

Let's define the top three things that are limiting your agency's growth today and determine which changes are possible in the next 90 days.

In this call, we will review these three building blocks to improved profitability:

- Lead generation strategies to attract your soul-mate clients
- Sales tactics for improved conversion
- Operational blocks that are keeping you stuck in the day-to-day

To create your three-step action plan now, click this link: creativeagencysuccess.com/startnow

PART TWO

Converting Prospects Into Paying Clients

CHAPTER 5

Sales Theory and How to Build Relationships

Many agency owners have a scary belief: that the agency must do whatever the client wants to make the sale. This doesn't even relate to the issue of being a generalist. No, you can have an entirely specialized agency with a well-defined niche and still fall into the same trap.

What often happens with agencies is that they take every request each client makes. Over time, they end up being everything for everybody within their market. Worst of all, agency owners don't even realize how this is hurting them.

Think back to the comparison we made between the used car salesperson and the Aston Martin dealer. Now, imagine that you come to that Aston Martin dealer and tell them that you want a minivan – and they start making one for you. Doesn't sound very likely, does it?

The same applies to your agency. Just as you don't want to be a jack of all trades in general, you don't want that to happen in your relationship with clients. Ultimately, taking on every role that your clients may need you to play will tie up your resources and production and damage your brand.

However, we need to clarify one thing here. Once you establish yourself as an expert in your niche, clients will likely start coming to you for various problems that fall outside of your chosen specialization. And that's a good thing.

But just because clients come *asking* for extra services doesn't mean you have to *accept* that kind of work.

The fact is, in the long run, you can make more money out of the nine deals that you don't do than the one you do. Not being contactable has an enormous value which you should never underestimate, and it's the same with saying *No*.

Your process starts with prospecting and establishing a relationship with a client. That's the initial point where you need to stay in control of the conversation and, rather than giving in to various client requests, assure them of success.

If you can do that right, you'll create a healthy foundation for that relationship, and that's a far more important thing than giving in to any potential whims the client might have. You should always listen to what the prospect has to say but not jump into action at every comment they make.

Ultimately, the prospect wants to feel safe with your agency and get the end result they need. And the best way to go about it isn't through creating a situation in which you're taking orders from them. It's through consulting with the prospect and challenging them with constructive advice based on your experience and expertise. This will create more trust and attachment than going along with everything the prospect suggests.

Of course, how you position yourself initially will depend on your mindset around sales.

Prospects will often try to take control away from you and take command of the conversation. This is a natural and respectable thing, but it works both ways. As soon as you take control back, you'll earn respect from that prospect if you do it the right way.

Taking back control of the conversation doesn't have to be a domineering act or a fake, orchestrated thing. It should be a gesture that shows this is *your* sales meeting and *your* agency. You're offering help to the prospect.

If you approach the conversation from that mindset, you'll ensure that your process remains your own. But you'll also make your prospects trust you more and feel comfortable about working with you. This is because people don't necessarily want to be in control themselves – they want to know that *someone's* in control, able to help them and that they are safe. Your clients need guidance and security, and you can show them that they can get all that in you if you act with conviction, commitment, and confidence.

There are different ways in which you could start building a relationship with your clients. While some elements, such as taking control and assuring your clients of success, are necessary, that doesn't mean there's only one way to do things.

In fact, you could be one of the four types of salespersons that can establish a successful relationship with their clients. Before moving forward, it would be best to determine which type fits you the best.

The Four Types of Salespersons

"Always enter the conversation already occurring in the customer's mind."

– Dan Kennedy

1. *Persistent*
Persistence is very important in sales but not in the way that people might think. For the majority of people, the first thing that comes to mind when they hear about a persistent salesperson is those telemarketers who keep trying to sell to you even after you've told them *No*.

Obviously, that's not the kind of persistence that you should show. If a prospect rejects your offer, you must accept it and move on. Understand it as that prospect not being the right fit to convert and realize that it wouldn't be a good relationship even if you could convince them to work with you.

The good kind of persistence relates to following up on your prospects in a reasonable manner to make sure that you're staying in touch. That way, you'll nurture that relationship without coming across as pushy or overly salesy. In other words, a moderate amount of persistence can go a long way, while going overboard won't bring results.

2. Knowledgeable

Being knowledgeable goes hand-in-hand with being specialized. When your clients know, feel, and recognize your expertise on a specific topic, they'll feel much safer with you.

Going to a knowledgeable salesperson is similar to going to a doctor. People know and trust someone who has studied medicine more than what they read on Web MD, and that comes down to the level of expertise that the real doctor possesses.

As this type of salesperson, you can allow people to relax and rely on your knowledge, which is an excellent way to establish a relationship. The more you invest in your specialization, the better you'll fulfill this role for your clients.

3. Passionate

This is a type of salesperson that people don't give enough credit to, and it's the type that gets really excited about what they do. Of course, the excitement isn't around making the sale but rather the subject of the conversation.

Someone who loves what they're talking about will make the prospect hyped about it, too. If you can get your prospects excited to get to the end goal that they're looking for, you'll pique their interest in the project.

Passion is very hard to create if it isn't there to begin with, which might be why this type of salesperson is often overlooked. However, if you specialize and niche down the right way, you'll likely end up doing something that you really love and that can turn you into a passionate salesperson.

4. Advisor

People don't want to hire someone that's at the same level as them. What they want is someone with more experience or additional knowledge.

When you take the position of a consultant or advisor in the conversation, you can immediately elevate yourself to that higher level. As the advisor type, you'll be asking more questions and giving slight pieces of advice.

However, the important part about the advice you give is to provide the *what* without the *how*. Because if you start giving your prospects the how, the first thing most of them will try is to do the process without you. Then, they'll inevitably mess it up, and you'll end up doing them a disservice.

The Foundations of a Sales Relationship

Once you've determined which type of salesperson you want to be, it's time to start laying down the foundations of your relationship with the client.

As with any other relationship, the vital thing is being yourself. We know when people aren't genuine, so being straightforward and true while building rapport is essential. If you start the relationship this way, you'll make every further interaction with the client easier.

In essence, building a relationship is all about trust, and to be true to your clients, you'll have to be true to yourself. However, there's something about building trust that people often don't recognize:

It's not about what you say, and it's not even about you. When you're building a trusting relationship, the crucial thing is that the other person understands that you care about them. That's what makes someone trust and like you, and that's what establishes the foundation of your connection to them.

Unfortunately, the wrong way to go about it is something that we see happen more frequently than not. It's when you meet someone new at a bar, bookshop, or wherever, and all they do is talk about themselves.

The person is telling you about all the things they've done, where they've been, and what they've accomplished in their lives. *And they don't ask you a single question.*

If you were in such a situation, how much would you be interested in that person? Probably not very much.

On the other hand, how would you react if the person asked you questions and showed that they wanted to learn about you and get to know you?

Your reaction would likely be much more favorable.

Now, think about a sales conversation in the same terms.

On the one side, you have a salesperson who comes in and starts telling you about their product – let's say it's a camera. They break it down to the smallest detail, explaining the depth of field, number of megapixels, and all the other cool features. They tell you how much better that camera is compared to other brands. Somewhere along the way, you start feeling that this salesperson is only interested in the product and making the sale, and you know that they don't really care about what you need.

On the other side, a different salesperson comes in with the same camera, but they don't discuss its features. Instead, they ask you, *"What would you like to use this camera for? Do you like taking photos of your family, landscapes, or something else?"*

Then, depending on your answer, the salesperson tells you how the camera can best serve your purpose.

This approach works much better because the salesperson is actually getting to know *you*. As a result, you start trusting them a bit more, and a relationship starts to form.

When you build a foundation, you'll want to be like that second salesperson. Start the conversation by considering what your prospects really want or need and use your expertise to make recommendations. Let the prospect talk and ask questions.

In fact, you can use a general guideline for your sales conversations:

First of all, there's something of a rule about how much talk should come from your side. If you've spoken for more than 30% of the conversation, you've most likely lost the sale.

If you want to distribute that 30%, here's a sequence outline that you can use:

Initially, you'll want to establish your authority and control in the conversation. Then, take an interest in your prospect and allow them to connect. At this point, you should show them that they're in the right place and make them feel safe and comfortable.

Once you get there, let the prospect tell you why they need your help, and only then go ahead and explain what you can do for them.

If you structure the conversation this way, by the end, both your client and you will have a clear idea about the relationship you're forming. But that won't only be an opportunity for the client to decide whether they want to work with you. It will also be the point at which you determine if the prospect is the right fit for your services.

New Client Qualification

"Once we learn to shun the non-believers, to be comfortable enough to say 'it's not for you,' then we free ourselves up. No one can make something for everyone."

– Seth Godin

Learning to say *No* is one of the most important aspects of building relationships as well as businesses. In other words, you'll need to qualify clients to ensure that they fit in with what you have to offer.

This decision can only come from a mindset that you're the prize. You provide the value, and your clients need you – not the other way around. When you realize that, you can start applying the client qualification process.

When qualifying clients, it's essential to have a set of requirements in place. You need to establish specific thresholds and make sure that your relationship with a client doesn't cross them.

The set of parameters for prospects to become clients should start with knowing who you want to work with. The first thing you should look for is whether you'll enjoy helping that particular person with your service. Ask yourself if you're excited about working with that client on achieving their goals. And if the answer to that question is *No*, that should also be your answer to the prospect.

Secondly, you'll want to ensure that you know what the prospect wants and that you can deliver what they need. If those two things don't fit together, you shouldn't take on that client. In fact, declining such clients will be mutually beneficial.

You won't burden yourself with a request that you can't meet, and the prospect will know they should look for the solution to their problem elsewhere.

Finally, establishing boundaries to what you can and can't or won't do is incredibly useful. This doesn't need to result in declining the prospect altogether. You can simply refer them to another way to get a particular thing done while keeping the piece of business that you can do well.

All of these are the ways in which you'll benefit from learning to say *No*. It's not about rejecting prospects as much as it's about setting thresholds to ensure that the relationships you build are created on a clear and firm foundation.

Establishing Authority

We've previously discussed the importance of building authority as the key to making sales. But that's not the only vital role that authority plays – it's also a crucial element in your relationships with clients.

One of the aspects that we've touched upon in the previous chapter was control over the conversation. In terms of building a relationship, this is something you can apply by handling objections properly.

This is very similar to what happens when parents talk to their kids and tell them, *"No, you can't do that. You're not allowed to."*

The first thing kids will feel in that case is that they'll want to do it even more.

The same happens with your clients. They might think that something would work great for them, but you know that it won't. If you simply tell them that, they'll likely feel resistance, and your relationship will be off to a rough start.

This isn't because clients are really like children. It's because most of them aren't used to hearing *No*, especially in a sales conversation, and it will hit them hard.

If you want to handle objections in a way that will help you build authority, you'll need to learn to say *No* to the client's ideas that don't work and help them understand the reason behind your answer.

This way of handling objections is something you should do genuinely. If you act that way, you'll immediately take the client into a place where they'll feel more endeared to you, and you'll elevate yourself within your relationship.

The next element of authority is to be relaxed. If you think about the times when you were most nervous, you'll find that those were situations when you were at the edge of your comfort zone.

But if you're an expert at what you do, you shouldn't have a reason to be stressed. People can easily pick up on whether you're relaxed or not. If you are, you'll instill confidence in your prospect and make them feel that they're in the right place. But if you feel unsettled or uncomfortable, your prospects will feel that way, too.

Again, this isn't something you should put on as an act. When you're having a conversation with a prospect, you should be genuinely relaxed because you've specialized, and you know what you're doing and understand your own worth as an expert.

The wrong way to enter a relationship with your clients is to anxiously seek their approval. Instead, you should adopt a mindset that you're the one determining whether the client is a good fit for your services.

If you come into the relationship with that attitude, you'll never come off as desperate or pushy. Rather, you'll remove all nervousness, and that'll further boost your authority.

Finally, as a person of authority, you should always listen to your prospects. When you're going through a sales conversation, you should ask them questions frequently and spend the majority of the time exploring what their issues, frustrations, and goals are.

There are two main reasons why listening is important. The first is, of course, that you'll understand what you need to solve much more clearly. But the second reason goes back to building your authority.

When you ask questions and listen, you're letting the prospect explain all of the reasons why they should work with you. In other words, you're letting them tell you how to sell to them. Then, the prospect is doing all the selling themselves, and all you have to do is take them through that journey.

In terms of authority building, you're not the one reaching out and telling the prospect what they want to hear in this scenario. You're also avoiding positioning yourself as someone who's taking orders. Instead, you're taking on the role of a consultant, advisor, and partner to your prospect.

You might wonder what the difference is between letting the prospect answer your questions and, as we just put it, taking orders. Well, in one case, you're the expert who is asking about their problems and telling them what the possible solutions are.

In the other case, you're letting the prospect tell you what specific solutions they're looking for. For example, if you're asking the prospect what types of ads they want to run, or if they want to target a specific demographic, you're doing it wrong.

Coming up with the exact solution for a problem is your job and yours alone. Of course, you should hear out what ideas your prospects might have. And then, you should teach them why their solutions aren't optimal and show them the right way to move forward. This will only boost the trust they have in you further.

After all, if your prospects knew what the solution was, they wouldn't need your help. That's why you should always direct the conversation towards their issues and make sure that you're the one explaining the way to resolve them.

Establishing authority right from the start will determine the entire dynamic of your relationship with the client. If you cover all of the key aspects that we've discussed here, you'll create a good foundation that will prove beneficial for everyone moving forward.

However, this will be much more challenging to do if you have to improvise the conversation every time. That's why you'll need to create some consistency in this process. You'll need a script.

Why You Need to Have a Script

When we talk about having a script, we're not referring to something like a movie script where you have every sentence you'll say written down. Rather, what you need is a process that will ensure that you do everything in a regimented way.

Your script will need to outline the questions that you'll ask and things you'll do during the conversation so that you can take every prospect through the same experience. When you create such an outline, you'll get a repeatable process that you can adjust and improve along the way.

While you should make the experience curated, it's worth mentioning that it doesn't need to be too strict. As you follow your script, you should never feel rigid and constricted by it. In this regard, your script doesn't have to be a detailed map of the conversation but rather a way to understand all of the essential points you should cover.

You should create a consistent process that will define the experience and the emotional impact you want to make. Coming up with this process is vital because it'll allow you to refine and improve your sales at every stage. This gives you the opportunity to fine-tune through trial and error questions that drive the conversation in certain ways.

When you start following a script, you'll develop a keen understanding of where the lowest-hanging fruit is in your sales process, as well as what part of the process is blocking your progress. Then, you'll be able to determine potential problems and fix them, which can bring massive benefits.

In fact, if you can make just a 2% increase at every stage of your funnel and sales process, you could almost double your revenue.

With a script at hand, you'll quickly discover a decent number of small leverage points in your sales calls. Then, you can optimize them to create a greater impact.

In terms of fixing problems, you'll find out which parts of the conversation have proven the most challenging. You'll notice that everything seemed fine up until you touched upon a certain point in the script. But when you started talking about that point, you had people disenchanted.

Determining these blockages in your sales process will be invaluable. You might find that you're saying something that doesn't resonate the right way and that you're losing rapport due to wording and the way you're phrasing the point in question.

Once you understand what's wrong, you can adjust, tweak, and optimize specific parts of your script. With each improvement, your script will become more reliable until you get a dependable process that works.

You Are the Prize

Doing sales right represents more than just making the prospect buy your service. It's a matter of building relationships and creating partnerships.

As an agency owner, you'll never be a typical salesperson. Of course, you'll want to increase your revenue and grow your business, but the crux of the process will always be that you're providing solutions and helping people.

This is the essential thing you should keep in mind. Your clients need you to solve their problems, and your service is precious to them. That's why you'll have to build a sales process that reflects all of the value you're bringing to the table and positions you as an expert who holds authority.

When you form the relationships in sales on that foundation, you'll establish a dynamic that will allow you to deliver your service in the most beneficial way for your agency and your clients.

Of course, tailoring your sales process in the most efficient way won't be easy. You'll need to work out every step thoroughly and deliberately and be mindful of the details that can make or break the sale.

Gift #3 - Value Pricing Guide

Are you eager to finally start charging for the full value you provide and earning your worth?

To bridge that gap, you'll need to make the following changes:

- Optimize your pricing with the fixed value-based pricing model.
- Communicate the value of your agency to your clients effectively.
  - Incorporate accurate financial reporting and project reviews.

You'll learn how to do all that (and more) via our guide:
creativeagencysuccess.com/resources

CHAPTER 6

Creating the Pitch

We all had that one teacher in school whose classes sent us to sleep.

You know the kind we're talking about. The subject they teach isn't necessarily boring, and they certainly have the qualifications and knowledge. But the way they talk and the energy they radiate make you want to doze off.

These teachers would state facts in a monotone voice and absolutely no presence. And it was no wonder that all of the students would check out after the first few minutes, learning nothing in the process.

If you've been really unfortunate, you might've had several teachers like this in your life. But you were probably lucky enough to have teachers with charisma and passion who engaged the whole class in an instant.

Students would come out of those classes in an entirely different way. They would pick up some knowledge and perhaps even grow to love the subject. The effective teacher may not have been as qualified as the boring one – the point is that they knew how to communicate the information and engage the students.

By now, you've probably realized what we're hinting at with the teacher story and how it relates to sales.

If you make your sales presentation an hour-long bore-fest of bombarding potential clients with facts and figures, all you'll do is send them to sleep. Because it's not about how accurate your information is but how you present it.

No one will care how clever or qualified you are or how much knowledge and expertise you have if you can't convey it all in a meaningful and beneficial way.

That's why you need to create an effective and engaging pitch. In this chapter, we'll show you how to do just that.

> "You are probably better than me, but do you know why I am going to get the job and you aren't?
>
> People like me, people want to be around me."
>
> – Unknown

Building a Capabilities Deck

The best way to ensure that your prospects aren't bored is to build an effective capabilities deck. This is a list of short, snappy points that will engage the prospect and flesh out how your service relates to their wants and needs.

The capabilities deck will serve as an outline for your pitch that you'll be able to use with every prospect. Once you build this deck, all you'll need to do will be to make slight adjustments to fit your prospect's needs.

Before we get into the capabilities deck, we should mention a crucial principle concerning the length of your pitch.

You'll want to limit yourself to 15 minutes or less. By restricting the pitch and making it shorter, you'll make it really concentrated and focused on nothing but the important stuff.

Here's what you need to get into those 15 minutes:

1. Why should the prospect care
2. Why you matter
3. How you can help
4. What services you offer and what your process is
5. The results you provide
6. Why do you do what you do

7. Case studies or social proof

The purpose of your pitch is to take your prospect on an emotional journey that depicts where they are and how they fit into your agency and preps them for the sale.

You'll need to establish authority and make the prospect care about what you have to say. You'll accomplish this by ensuring that they feel they're in the right place and talking to the right people.

Then, you'll explain what the components of the process are from the side of your agency. This includes your mindset, the theory behind how you execute and deliver, and the way that you make it happen in practice.

This part is important because it communicates to the prospect that they aren't your guinea pig. You've done this type of work before, and you have a reliable, repeatable process. That they can trust you.

Moving forward, you'll need to explain what your services entail to reinforce the idea of your expertise and specialization. This will also set the expectations for the results.

Of course, you won't talk about your process in great detail. Instead, you'll provide enough explanation so that the prospect buys into it and doesn't want you to move outside that process.

By showing them exactly how you deliver results, you'll simultaneously teach the prospect all they need to know about the solutions you offer and ensure that they feel you're the right choice.

From here, you can move into case studies to illustrate the results that your agency can provide. Finally, you'll get to the testimonials and social proof that will showcase how you've been able to help other people accomplish their goals.

The key thing about presenting your capabilities deck is to approach it with the right mindset. You don't want to deliver your pitch like you're selling, but add some swag to it.

It would be best not to think about it as pitching at all. Think about how you're telling the prospect about the things you've done and how you did it.

Be relaxed about it and simply present your agency as the phenomenal thing that it is. However, don't lose sight of your prospect's needs and how what you do relates to their issues.

If you deliver your capabilities deck effectively, you'll be able to move directly into a strategy session or a discovery call.

Effective Discovery Calls

A discovery call is one of your opportunities to build rapport even further. It's where you dig deeper into your prospects' challenges and work out how you'll resolve them.

Sometimes, the discovery call isn't about what you say at all but how you say it. Your tone and how you present yourself can make all the difference because you're still leading the prospect through the journey that started with your pitch.

If you want to set the purpose and the feel of the discovery call right, you'll need to approach it from an angle that will make the call as effective as possible. And you'll do that by working out the following key points.

It Doesn't Need to Feel Icky

Most agencies have a particular lifecycle that doesn't set them up for sales very well. You might've started out doing freelance work and got very good at it. Then, as time went by, the number of your clients grew, and you had to hire an employee.

After some time, you got even more clients, which meant you needed more employees, and you ended up starting a full-fledged agency.

The issue is that no one in your team ever enjoyed sales or received any training in it. As a result, you might still be in the mindset that, if you're to be a salesperson, you have to embody that used car salesman type mentioned in previous chapters.

In fact, many agency owners describe sales as making them feel icky. But it really doesn't have to be like that.

Sales is about connecting, having a conversation, and helping someone else. And when you have a discovery call, this is the approach you'll need to take because that's when the sale happens. There's no attempt to trick anyone. You aren't pulling one over on your prospects – you're only interested in exploring something that's mutually advantageous.

You need to understand that your clients will buy into your process during the discovery call, not the proposal. That's why it's important to change your mindset about sales from the very start.

You aren't forcing a decision on your clients, and you aren't doing the call out of desperation to sell. You're creating a bridge between your agency and the client that will allow you to provide a unique solution to the thing that's keeping them down.

The Importance of Being Personable While Connecting With Them

Creating a genuine connection with the client will also depend on your mindset. As you're presenting your service, you should do it from the point of understanding your client's struggles. After all, that's the main purpose of your offer and the discovery call.

Your default viewpoint should always be that you're still building the relationship. Converting prospects into clients is important, but it will only benefit you and them if you create a connection and genuinely approach the conversation.

This aspect might seem straightforward and self-explanatory, but it's easy to forget if you happen to slip back into the stereotypical sales mindset. Maintain your focus on the person you're talking with and keep their needs and goals in mind.

Allow Them to Sell Themselves

The discovery call is the ideal time for you to curate the experience for the potential client to sell themselves.

You'll ask them questions about what they're looking for and what they want to get out of it. Throughout that process, the client will start to recognize that you're exactly who they need to help them achieve what they want.

This way, your prospects will realize their ultimate goals and that the solution they need is in your agency. In the end, you won't have to do much selling at all. The client will get to that point on their own.

Asking About Budget

When you get clarity on what your clients need and how you'll provide the results, the question of the budget will need to come up.

This is a crucial thing that many agencies struggle with because they believe that getting a number is almost impossible. However, you can find that information out if you set up the conversation properly.

The way to do that is by starting the discovery call with a question:

"Are you okay having a detailed conversation about your business today?"

Of course, the client will say that they are okay with that and give you permission to ask them various questions. With that permission, you'll be able to ask about their budget.

When talking about the budget directly, you should ask what their budget was last year rather than ask about the current situation. The majority of people will have no problem sharing that information. Even if they refuse, you can remind them that they said it was okay to have a detailed conversation.

It's also useful to acknowledge that many people don't like answering this question, but it would be a great way to understand where your client is. Asking about the budget is how you can ensure that your services can bring the clients the best ROI, and that's something you should let them know.

If you feel nervous about asking the budget question, keep in mind that you're not asking about private information, even though it might seem that way. You're trying to find out what you're working with so that you can maximize the results.

Nervous Nature of Creatives Selling Themselves

Sales is often seen as an activity for extroverted people, which can discourage many creatives when selling themselves. However, if you're an introvert, it doesn't mean that you don't have what it takes.

If you talk to our clients today, all of them would say that Robert Patin is a natural at sales. And yet, that's not who I was to begin with. In fact, I've been introverted for most of my life, a textbook nerd.

I've always been an analytical, straight-to-the-point person, but I didn't really truly socialize until my mid-20s. Then, I started becoming a bit more social and believing in myself and, finally, discovered a part of my personality that was actually very charismatic.

The thing that switched everything around and allowed me to present that charismatic side might sound ridiculous, but it worked.

Before every sales meeting, I would stand in a Superman pose for about five minutes and tell myself that I'm awesome, and I'm going to nail it. Then, when I'd start feeling emboldened and stronger, I'd get into the meeting room.

I told you it would sound ridiculous!

But the fact is that doing this helped me become better and more confident. But I wasn't just getting better in sales – I was becoming *me* more and more.

Being extroverted isn't a thing that you have to put on as an act. It's about letting your true *you* get through, regardless of what anyone thinks of it. When you get into a discovery call, you won't need to "turn on" some special power to be genuine and charismatic. Just be who you are.

Gaining Conceptual Buy-In

The ultimate point of a discovery call is for you to gather information and let the client tell you why they need you. As they're going through that experience, they'll start gaining the conceptual buy-in.

The client will explain why they need you, and you can guide them along by dropping in little nuggets of expertise. Then you can start to nurture and grow the client's buy-in with more pieces of information at different stages.

It's like you're showing the prospect the answer to all their questions and then putting it back in your pocket. This way, you'll warm them up and strengthen the connection without giving them too much material to handle.

It's Simpler Than It Seems

You should always keep in mind that the entire sales process is essentially about building a relationship. It's not as complex as it seems because you've been building relationships since childhood.

Just as you've connected with people and made them like you, your agency can do the same. There's no reason to build the process up in your head and make it overwhelming. Keep it simple and remember that all you're really doing is connecting to another person who needs your help.

Don't Be Too Eager

There's a principle that can help you significantly in sales:

The person who loves the least is the one that gets pursued the most.

Of course, this doesn't mean you should actively try to appear uninterested. Instead, the principle is about dialing yourself back just a little and transferring the dynamic so that the client's more interested in what you have to offer.

Refraining from appearing too eager isn't just a matter of appearance but also a matter of fact. Remember, your prospects *do* need you more than you need them, and it's only natural that will make you more attractive to them.

Remove the Sale From the Sell

A story from Dale Carnegie's excellent book *How to Win Friends and Influence People* is very relevant to this point.

The story is about a family with two children where the younger kid didn't want to go to school. Rather than ordering the child to go regardless of how they felt, the parents decided to handle the situation differently.

They told the kid to go and get ready for bed, and then they sat down with the older sibling and started doing finger-painting and other fun stuff.

The younger child heard them and came to ask if they could join in with the fun. At that point, the parents said that only kids who've gone to school could do that stuff. The result was, of course, that the kid eagerly went to school the next day.

You can apply the same mentality to sales. You don't need to force your prospects into working with you. All you need to do is remove the sales part from the sell and present them with the awesome things that will come if they take you up on your offer.

The Seven Commandments of Discovery Calls

Finally, there are seven strict rules that you should always apply to your discovery calls. We call them "The Seven Commandments of Discovery Calls," and they're straightforward principles that don't require explanation:

1. Have all stakeholders on the call
2. Do not lie
3. Do not overpromise
4. Do not oversell
5. Do not sell to someone you can't help
6. Do not sell what will not help
7. Your obligation is to sell to your prospects what will help them accomplish their goals

Keep these seven commandments in mind. Don't break them under any circumstances, and make them the core of your discovery calls.

A Word on RFPs

There's a process that might take place when your potential client is a large company – a request for proposal or RFP.

Typically, this is a structured process that allows big companies to get multiple proposals from different sides and discount the price as much as possible. We aren't huge fans of RFPs for several key reasons.

First, the negotiation that happens around an RFP doesn't necessarily lead to your agency getting any business. The goal of the process is for the large company to get a service that's cheaper than the incumbent agency, possibly even merely looking to get that agency to discount their current fees.

As a result, when you get an RFP, you'll likely spend a lot of time preparing and figuring out your proposal, talking to the company, and submitting all of the necessary paperwork. However, in most cases, you won't get the business.

This is the downside of working with potential enterprise clients that many agencies aren't aware of. But the second reason why we don't like RFPs might sound even worse.

Even if you get the job with an enterprise client, there's a real possibility that your creative license will be limited and you'll become burdened by company procedures. However, it's worth noting that not every enterprise client will be like that.

The bottom line of RFPs is that you should be careful when responding to them and do thorough research before engaging with that type of client. Make a calculated decision and ensure that the business you get is worth it.

If you go about this carefully, you might end up striking gold. But if you start responding to RFPs without such considerations, you'll likely just end up losing time and energy.

Engaging Pitches Convert Clients

By now, it should be clear that your pitch and discovery calls have a clear purpose in making it possible to reach clients and help them. If you've adopted that mindset and accepted sales as the positive process it is, you're already on the right path.

The way your agency grows and scales will largely depend on your sales techniques and how much you focus on what your prospects need. If you want to get the opportunity to engage new clients and provide them with the best results through your services, you'll need to master sales first.

A great deal of planning goes into nailing the pitch and coming up with an ideal discovery call plan. However, once you have those elements in place, your agency will be ready to start scaling and fulfill its purpose.

Gift #4 - Guide on Capabilities Presentations

The ability to deliver a truly engaging pitch is the foundation of your relationship with clients. As such, it would be best to master this art as soon as possible.

Here are the skill sets you need to do that:

- Create presentations that convert.
- Incorporate new and innovative ways to engage prospects. •
  Elevate your authority in 15 minutes or less.

Download your free copy of our guide to learn how to do all this (and more):

CHAPTER 7

The Art of the Close

There's an unfortunate trend in Hollywood blockbusters lately.

When a new movie is about to be released, there's all this hype with marketing and trailers that get people very excited. For a few weeks or even months, everybody's talking about when the movie will hit theaters and streaming services, and fans are going crazy counting down to the premier.

Finally, the flick starts showing, and audiences flock to see the mindbending masterpiece they've been promised...

Only to be left utterly disappointed.

If you have seen a so-called blockbuster in the last decade, you have probably experienced this.

These are the type of movies where all of the best scenes are already in the trailer. But when you watch the whole thing, it turns out those scenes were the *only* thing worth watching. Sure, these flicks raked in a lot of money, but they certainly didn't live up to the hype created around them. In fact, after letting down such a huge number of fans, they more likely spelled doom for the franchises than managed to uplift them.

And worst of all, maybe those movies would've had a better reception if not for the marketing presenting them as the best thing since sliced bread.

There's an apt analogy here. Movie marketing is much the same as making a sales pitch and outreaching, and the premier can be compared to closing the deal.

Everything you do up to the close is the build-up, just like a movie trailer.

When the moment actually comes to close the deal, you must ensure that it doesn't make the whole thing fall flat.

The way you close will be critical to all that you have done so far. And in this chapter, you will learn how to ensure the whole process ends up a success.

The Timeline for the Close

When it comes to the close, the vital point is that you have set certain expectations, and now you need to stick to them.

This concept extends to the meeting. People need to know what to expect from you throughout the entire process.

If you have built up everything you can do, what your capabilities are, and what you can deliver, it would be very detrimental to get to the meeting and back down on those expectations.

You do not want to end up in such a situation. That's why following up on the expectations you have created is paramount, but there's more that goes into creating a successful close.

Another crucial principle with closure is: the sooner, the better.

When in meetings, never give people too much time to think. Same as you wouldn't want to talk yourself out of a sale, you shouldn't give the prospect the opportunity to do so, either.

This is where the timeline of the close comes in. It is best to have it structured and be very specific about it. Keep in mind that the more downtime you give to a prospect, the more likely it will be for them to overthink it.

The key thing about structuring the close is to let the prospect know what you will be talking about and set up the following meetings. Again, you need to set expectations and follow them through.

For example, you could say that you will give them the contract on Monday, then set up a meeting to go over it on Wednesday, and have a follow-up meeting on Friday.

What you shouldn't do is just send the proposal and let the prospect know that you will meet them to talk about it or leave it to them to get back to you.

Another thing you definitely shouldn't do is get too specific with the timeline, describing what the meeting will look like from one minute to the next.

Have a clear outline, set the expectations, and let the actual conversation progress so that it feels organic.

Regarding those expectations, you should always aim for the so-called *BAMFAM* – Book a Meeting from a Meeting. This lines up with the example we made. Instead of sealing the deal in a single conversation, create a progression from one meeting to another.

This approach will allow you to structure the close and cover the crucial principles within the timeline.

When you are moving into the close, there's one red flag that should always grab your attention. It often happens when agencies make proposals: the client starts saying what they want, and the agency gives in on every request rather than pushing back, establishing themselves as the advisor.

This approach can lead to many issues, from the client developing unrealistic expectations to the agency suffering from scope creep and eventually not delivering the best results.

One of our clients had a brilliant way of dealing with this problem.

When a prospect asked them to complete a project in a specific timeframe, they returned with a timeframe that was twice as long and a price that surpassed the prospect's budget four times.

The prospect was taken aback. They replied, *"We said that we needed it to be done in three months."*

Our client said: *"Would you prefer to have our first idea or our best idea? With the timeline that you outlined, we would only have time for the first idea. We do not believe that is the best way forward, so we have presented you with a timeline that would allow for the best results. Any agency that suggests that they can do it in your timeline will be providing you with their first idea."*

The way our client handled this situation covered a great number of potential issues. Through one response, they dealt with the objection, negated competitors, gained credibility, and pushed back against the prospect, which garnered more respect.

Reacting promptly to objections will set the tone for the follow-up meetings, reaffirm expectations, and allow you to stick to the plan and maintain the timeline for the close.

And all of that will depend on how you deliver your proposal.

Stop Emailing Your Proposals Now

Emailing your proposal is the number one mistake I see agencies regularly make in sales.

There's zero excitement to it – no pizzazz, no objection management, no charisma, nothing.

It is like getting your audience hyped for a movie and then giving them a bootleg version to watch over their phone.

As a result, it becomes easier for clients to reject your proposal and misinterpret or even overlook the value of your service. All of the passion and engagement we have talked about previously will simply evaporate if you wrap it up with an email proposal.

If you want to create the best opportunity for a close, you should get in front of your clients. Then, you can address any initial objections and enhance the entire experience.

When you deliver your proposal through a call, you can remind the client why they started talking with you in the first place, remind them of their need or "why." Many things could happen between the last conversation you had with the client and the time you make the proposal. That's why you need to reconnect with them and refresh the trust that you have already built.

Remember, you have gained the client's conceptual buy-in during the discovery call. That was when the majority of the sale happened. In other words, your proposal is not about selling because that part was already covered.

When it comes to the close, you should re-establish the connection with the client because that connection is what sells. You should remind your client of what they described, reconnect them to the feeling that they had in prior meetings, manage any objections, and provide them the cost.

And, as we stated, it is much easier for them to say *No* if you provide your proposal via email. In sales, everything's about connection, the relationship you build, and the emotion. When you email your proposal, you do not get any of that.

On the other hand, in a live conversation, you can ensure that your client remembers the relationship that was established around their need and your ability to deliver.

You will do that more easily if you follow the five key principles of closing.

The Five Principles of Closing

Because most of the sale happens previous to the close, a lot of what you will talk about with the client will be about reiterating the points you have made earlier. However, there are certain beats you will need to hit precisely to really drive the conversation home. Pay attention to these principles, and you will make the close go much smoother.

1. Reaffirm the Need

Reaffirming the client's need is pretty much self-explanatory, but it is also a critical factor. This is the point at which you are reminding the client why they're here.

You should start with talking about why the client called you and that you described to them how you could deliver on their needs. In essence, you should reiterate the same things that you have gone over before.

However, there's more than repeating everything the client told you in the previous meeting back to them when it comes to this principle. You can make it more detailed.

One great way to do so is by creating a pseudo-consultative experience by highlighting the client's needs with different colors.

For example, you could create a chart and assign a color for the level of help they need with different aspects of their work. Green could be for things your client can handle themselves and red for those only you could resolve.

In the vast majority of cases, the chart will be mostly red by the time you are done.

This is an excellent visual representation that will remind the client how much they need your help. It is also a great lead-in for the next principle, which will be all about their frustration.

2. Connect Their Frustration to Your Service

Once you have outlined the client's need, you should expand on the frustration that comes from having unresolved issues. When your client sees everything that needs to be done, they will remember precisely what their concerns and pain points are.

They will become more aware of the problems they're facing because those will be stated outright. At this point, it would be good to go over everything that might happen if the client's issues do not get fixed.

Then, once you have re-established the frustration, you can remind the client how your service relates to it. This conversation already took place before, so you do not have to emphasize the main points too much. And you certainly do not want to sound salesy.

The main thing you will want to achieve here is to bring up the main frustration and reinforce the idea that your service can help the client alleviate it.

Bring their existing position and emotion back to the surface.

3. It Is Riskier to Not Engage Than Engage

When talking about this principle, it is worth mentioning that you should position and frame it in a specific way.

While you want to get the point across that it is riskier for your client not to engage, you do not want to sound like you are using fear tactics or pressuring them into the close. After all, you have already brought up the critical matters by now.

Instead, you should focus on the benefits the client will get by working with you regarding their pain points. This is especially useful if you are doing a monthly retainer-type engagement.

Going by the color-coded example we mentioned earlier, you can show the client how you will handle the red areas first. Then, moving from those most demanding aspects to the green areas, explain what adjustments and improvements you could make even to the areas that the client believes are working just fine.

By showcasing how you will alleviate the pain and frustration, you will simultaneously point out why having your help will be less risky for the client than staying where they are.

You can emphasize this point further by exploring what your client is likely feeling right now about their future. However, do not linger on agitating the existing problems. you will want to remind them of the issues without making it feel raw, and you will do just that if you keep your focus on the solutions that you have got in store for them.

4. Maintain Excitement

Through the close, you should maintain a specific tone. On the one hand, you do not want the process to be just a pleasant experience that reassures the client that they're in the right place.

But on the other hand, you also do not want to create fear or uncertainty in their mind.

Your tone needs to convey the same level of excitement that you had during the discovery call. Drawing from the previous principle, you should get your client looking forward to awesome things to come and get them eager to engage fully as soon as possible.

Remember, this doesn't mean the same thing as selling to the client. Look at it like this:

Take Doubletree. You know the client's hungry, and you have already baked a tray of warm, tasty cookies for them. The cookies are ready, and you are willing to give them to the client – it is up to them to take up the offer. All you need to do in that regard is make sure that those cookies stay warm.

In other words, you have already built the excitement initially. During the close, you have to keep the client enthusiastic about the results they're about to get.

5. Proposals Aren't for Selling (They're for Detailing Scope)

The final principle has to do with the purpose of your proposal. While we have already established that the selling part has happened before, it is a point worth repeating and something you must always keep in mind.

However, that's only half of the story that explains what your proposal is not for. Let's look at what the goal *is*.

The closing conversation should deal in large part with detailing exactly what's included in your services and what is not. Both you and the client need to have a very clear understanding of the expectations and what you will be doing.

This is also about setting boundaries. You should bring up all of the details of what will be delivered and clarify the expectations for everything included and excluded from that delivery.

Handling Objections (and Why You Shouldn't Discount Your Services)

As you are working out the details of the deal, you will likely come upon certain objections. Most of the time, these will be related to how quickly you can get the project done, the scope of the work, or the price.

Even after you have precisely outlined everything you will do, the client might ask for some adjustments that fall outside of the boundaries you have set. In that case, it is crucial to handle such objections in a way that reaffirms your authority and the value of your service.

This is especially important when it comes to pricing. When clients have a very particular problem, and you have a specific way of resolving it, the scope and timing of your delivery will most likely be established well. And if any objections emerge that are related to that, you can handle them relatively easily.

Think back to the example of our client who pushed back on the prospect trying to rush the project.

Typically, when it comes to pricing, many agencies tend to give way to their clients' requests, discounting their services and setting a bad precedent. If a client asks you whether you could do the work for a lesser price and you agree to it, you will create certain expectations in their mind. In every subsequent case, the client may likely think that your price is not a solid number and that they could get another discount.

So, how do you answer if the client asks you to lower the price for a service?

You can say, *"Sure, no problem. What do you want us to leave out?"*

You should always keep in mind that your price is there for a reason. It is not just a number you have made up. It signifies the worth of your services and respect for their value. Through your actions, you will need to make prospective clients aware of that fact. Otherwise, they can actually deteriorate the quality of the relationship you are building with clients.

When you keep a fixed price for the service you provide, your relationship with the client is based on the value you provide. The conversation revolves around the quality of your service and the solutions you can offer while your pricing is set and unquestionable.

This way, you put yourself in a position where the uniqueness of your work is paramount.

In contrast, once you start giving discounts, the relationship starts revolving around the price, becoming transactional. These relationships will always collapse the moment somebody else comes by and offers a slightly better deal.

Through discounts, all you will do is devalue your service. Remember that you do not need extremely high closure rates, which means you do not have to change your offer just to make the client agree to your proposal.

What you want are clients who will pay what you are worth.

Master the Art

Now that you have read about everything that goes into a successful close, it should be clear that it is very much an art.

Closing the deal properly will require you to have a certain approach, plan out how you will time the meetings with clients and achieve complete clarity on the crucial aspects of the process.

Besides keeping to the key principles of the close and knowing *what* to talk about, you will also need to pay attention to *how* you conduct the conversation. In other words, the tone you establish will play a role in the outcome, too.

If you have done everything else right, the close will be about wrapping up and working out the details. Keep in mind the expectations you have created earlier in the process and stay true to them when making your proposal, and be careful not to create new, unrealistic expectations at the finish line.

Finally, it is important to repeat the point of handling objections and not agreeing on discounts. As you are getting ready to close the deal, be wary of creating precedents that might jeopardize your relationship with the client in the future.

Gift #5 - Resources to Help Take Your Agency to the Next Level

Progress often doesn't take the form of a smooth, linear line. There's always going to be some form of trial and error, two steps forward and one step back.

But you can help to streamline and accelerate the process by avoiding common setbacks. These are the areas where many agencies stumble:

- Building and delivering proposals in the right way.
- Scaling your agency smoothly and efficiently.
- Keeping up to date with the best industry practices and new developments.

If you need help with any of these, do check out the wealth of free resources we have here: https://www.creativeagencysuccess.com/resources

PART THREE

Delivering Amazing Results

CHAPTER 8

Client and Project Management

A few years ago, talk of a new, luxurious music festival shook the music industry.

The name of this event was "Fyre Festival," and it was founded by famous rapper Ja Rule and a man called Billy McFarland. It was supposed to be a huge deal, with the festival promotion promising attendees accommodation in lush villas on an island paradise in the Bahamas.

The festival was going to take place over two weekends during which people would enjoy top-class music acts while indulging their taste buds with gourmet meals.

However, while the marketing team kept promoting all of these splendors, many complications were going on behind the scenes. Yet, the organizers didn't mention anything going wrong.

As the Fyre Festival dates grew closer, people were already buying sixfigure tickets for the event. The festival was intended to promote a new app to streamline the booking process for rising music talents, talks about investments in the app were also underway.

Then, finally, the time came for the festival to start, and the first attendees arrived.

What they found wasn't the luxury featured in the promotional material that was flooding social networks.

Instead, people found themselves at a surprise beach party where they were supposed to wait for their accommodations to be ready.

Soon enough, it turned out there was no sign of the villas promised in the festival marketing. In their place, pre-packaged sandwiches and damp mattresses in tents, soaked from the recent rain.

The festival visitors learned that rather than an exotic beach, the festival proper was taking place on an abandoned development ground.

It didn't take long for the entire event to get officially canceled, and lawsuits against the organizers followed in the coming months. As a result, McFarland received a six-year prison sentence, and vast amounts of money were forfeited.

Worst of all, the Fyre Festival wasn't simply a con job done on unsuspecting patrons. It was a project that started with outrageous promises but couldn't deliver even a portion of them.

There's a valuable lesson here, and it has to do with managing projects and clients properly; before spiraling into a spectacle of disaster and fraud, the wrong steps taken by organizers started simply enough, as a cautionary tale of how unrealistic expectations can take on a momentum of their own.

If you want to deliver high value on what you promise, you will need to manage your client's expectations and your projects with utmost efficiency. In this chapter, you will learn how to do just that.

Framing Your Client's Expectations

The question of managing your client's expectations starts from the very beginning of your onboarding process.

While you have told the client what you are going to do in previous meetings, you will get into the details of how the rollout will happen once the actual onboarding begins.

This is the point where you set up the entire framework for everything you will deliver and put specific processes in place. But you will not do that part by yourself. Rather, your client will become an active part of that framework in the sense that the two of you will be getting the details worked out together.

In practice, it might look like this:

You will have a meeting with the client, explaining which deliverables they will receive by a certain date. Then, you will outline the rollout. During that meeting, you will clarify what your next actions will be, as well as what you will need from the client.

Then, you will continue to have similar meetings at the defined cadence.

This approach will help you solidify the expectations and deliverables. It will serve as a constant reminder for the client about the agreement you have reached at the start of the relationship in terms of how they will get to the outcome they want.

This is the main point of onboarding meetings. It is where you dot all of the I's and cross all of the T's. The goal is to cover every aspect thoroughly, ensuring that you and the client are on the same page in every regard.

Helping Clients Understand Your Processes

When it comes to explaining and defining your creative processes, a mindset issue often comes up.

You might think of creativity as a free-flowing, loose mindset of doing things. And that's partially true – as a creative, you do not know when you will get an idea and what's going to spark it. Furthermore, you might not know if you have got the best possible idea in the majority of cases.

However, this drives creative people to think that they do not like structure. This is fundamentally, biologically untrue. Humans as a species thrive in structure – we are the rules animal.

If you look at the very term "creative processes," it has the word "process" in the name. In other words, there's definitely a structure to creative work. And creative people are often more structured than others.

As a creative, you can thrive in a process-oriented environment, even though you might not realize the connection between it and your own creativity.

Documenting, defining, and allowing those processes to be replicated is critical to creative work. This is something you need to understand for yourself and explain to your clients.

It is best to start thinking about creating an assembly line-esque process for your work, which is something you can also guide your clients through. It doesn't have to be an overly massive, finely orchestrated thing.

In fact, in conversations about structure and processes, it is best to adhere to the KISS principle. Keep it as simple as possible and break it down in a detailed fashion to the most simplistic step-by-step instructions.

This part is really important in terms of getting on the same page with your clients and framing their expectations. You need to show them that the methods and processes you are introducing are in line with your creative efforts.

In fact, you are setting up standards that will apply to both your agency and the client in terms of how everything else will function from that point onward.

Defining Communication Expectations

During the onboarding process, you will also need to set up the standards of communication. Many agencies make a mistake in that regard because they create certain expectations with their clients that the agency will respond to every email from them within an hour.

This ends up being a detriment to everyone. When an agency is constantly scrambling to reply to the client, those answers aren't well thought out and ultimately serve no purpose.

That's why you have to set the expectation that the client's emails will always be important and that you will get back to them. However, you need to make it clear that the reply might come later the same day or within 24 hours, not immediately after you have received the email.

Standards of communications such as this allow for more clarity both in how your internal team understands what the client should experience and in setting the client's expectations towards your agency.

Your onboarding process should also establish a timeline that your client will easily understand. Here, the main point is to remember that your client is not an expert in your processes. In other words, you will need to help them understand what you will do without any assumptions.

Define each step using simple, plain language so that everything from the client experience to your agency's standards is 100% clear.

Then, once these basics are covered, you can move on to the finer details of your relationship with the client.

Create a White Glove Service

A white glove service refers to building little things into the way you communicate, manage projects, and grow your client relationships. These are the details that will leave them smiling and have them remember you.

Think about sending birthday gifts that resonate with the individual client, something that shows you have listened and paid attention, and that you are interested in who they are as a person, not just as one of your clients.

And these can really be small things, not grand gestures. The main point is that these personal touches should always be about the client rather than about you.

For example, you could send something like branded mugs or similar items. But the branding should be of your client or something they care about, not of your agency; no one cherishes the free pen they get from their local bank branch.

But small tokens of appreciation can show the client that you are thinking about them. They also make your clients feel good about working with you and let them know that you are acting in favor of your relationship.

While this detail might seem like something that can be overlooked, it actually goes a long way. By maintaining this white glove service, you are building upon the rapport you have established earlier and taking the relationship with your clients to a different level.

People remember how they felt for a lifetime…

Learn to Say No

When you are interacting with a client, it can be really easy to start overpromising during the initial meetings. This can eventually lead to issues when you need to deliver on those promises. We've already seen how poorly that can go in the example of the Fyre Festival and the logistical nightmare that left attendees utterly disappointed.

After you have set up the framework and outlined all the important aspects, the client can come to you with some small requests. However, if you do not know how to manage them, those requests can start stacking up because it doesn't seem like a big deal to say yes to them individually.

Clients often act this way because they might not understand the exact scope of your work. And even if you explain everything to them in detail and put certain limitations in place, they might still come back with little requests.

That's where you have to remember the dangers of overpromising. If you cannot be sure you can deliver on something, you will need to say no to the client and explain why that's the case.

Many agencies have a fear of saying no because they think it will put them on bad terms with the client. In reality, when you decline a client request because it falls outside of the scope of what you can deliver, you will earn even more respect from them.

However, learning to say no is not just about having others respect you. It is primarily about having respect for yourself. When you determine your boundaries, you are making sure that you are holding yourself to a standard.

Your time is precious. It is important to show your clients that you respect yourself enough to have boundaries.

Scope Creep Management

Even if you do not take additional requests from clients, projects can quickly get bloated and surpass their original scope.

This can often happen because you want to help your clients as much as possible, but it leads to many issues, such as lowered profitability and the inability to produce quality results for the unrealistic expectations that you set.

Furthermore, many agencies keep the information about the project's goals and full scope from their creative and operation teams, which means that their teams can't be a part of the early warning system.

These factors allow for scope creep to get out of hand and endanger the entire project.

One of our clients had exactly that happen to their agency.

They were working with a client for a number of years, and during that time, the scope of their work kept slowly piling up. In fact, when we took a look at what they were doing at the time, it hardly resembled what they started from.

Initially, this agency was supposed to do creative design for their client. However, they ended up doing social media management, content and digital advertising, and a bunch of other stuff that grew the relatively small scope they started with into a behemoth of scope creep.

When the staggering difference in the agency's work became apparent to everyone, they concluded that the situation was in desperate need of some management. They ended up telling the client about everything they were doing and that they had to adjust the scope.

The agency then presented its client with a new price. And, of course, the client was furious. The agency had been doing all of that work for years and had only now accounted for it with a price four times larger than the initial fee.

In this case, the client actually had some reasonable cause to be upset; they'd become accustomed to how things functioned for a long time – the expectations from precedent were long set.

Resolving this situation took plenty of careful handling. We helped the agency craft an email that addressed every aspect.

In this email, the agency management explained one crucial thing: that they were wrong to have let the situation develop in this way. They acknowledged that they set the wrong expectations and that *they* went way outside of the scope. Further, that this approach led to years of mismanaging their account and that the situation had been completely unprofessional.

Despite acknowledging all of the above, the agency had to make changes. As much as their client wanted to make money, the agency needed to do the same.

The client responded, agreeing with what was brought up in the email and proposing to talk about the pricing.

As you can see, once your agency starts building scope creep, it can be challenging to account for it and set everything back on track. Worst of all, it can happen without anyone noticing the effect right away. Instead, you only become aware of it when it is almost too late – describing this as a creeping process is very apt.

This is why you need to think about scope creep before it happens. There needs to be processes in place that can alert management or project management that the work is reaching certain thresholds, safeguards to ensure a relationship remains profitable.

At the same time, your team needs to be aware of crucial project information and understand what success should look like and what the agreed scope of the project is. Making your team a part of an early warning system is one of the ultimate steps in dealing with the scope creep issue.

If you have such early warning systems in place, you can start making corrections. This starts as an internal process. However, once you figure out the necessary adjustments, you will need to let the client know about them.

The reason why you need to be careful with scope creep is that it can be a slippery slope. Your client might request to do something that falls outside of the work scope one time, and you might agree to it as a favor.

But if that happens, the client will most likely ask you to do the same thing again. After all, you did it the last time, so why wouldn't you do it once more?

This is when a simple favor can grow into scope creep and become a real problem. And in the long term, it is a sure way to turn your best clients into the absolute worst clients.

Yet, that doesn't mean you should never do favors for your clients. However, you must make it clear that, should they ask you to do something outside of the agreed work, it is a one-time thing, setting the right expectation. This can be as simple as saying, *"We're happy to help you out with X this time, although it is outside of our current scope."*

Eliminating Waste

Eliminating waste means pursuing a simplified process that allows you to automate delivery while reducing human error as much as possible.

You might start out with a single client, and everything might work just fine. That will not be the case when you have 50 clients. At that point, it becomes increasingly difficult to remember all of the details of timing and delivery.

In fact, the more clients you have, the more you will be prone to errors. That's precisely why you will need to create a dependable system around your delivery process. Then, every time something happens that's not according to plan, you can adjust a system in place to fix it.

When it comes to eliminating waste in this sense, everything will come down to systems and how you approach them.

Whenever possible, make sure that you do not have a single source of error for a particular task. For example, trading companies often adopt the four eyes approach, which means that a second person needs to verify trades that surpass a certain volume. Mistakes can be extremely costly – people have lost billions of dollars simply due to missing a trade.

In essence, you need to have a well-defined workflow with enough redundancies to ensure nothing slips through the cracks.

Besides these workflow improvements, you should keep checklists for all of the essentials. This is a simple technique that many workplaces employ to great effect. Even surgeons have checklists that ensure they've got the right patient ready for the right surgery. Adopting that mentality into your agency will certainly make a difference for the better when it comes to eliminating waste.

Furthermore, it is vital to have benchmarking data that allows you to compare one client to another. This will help you understand which projects were the most successful, and which were not. Making a comparison between them will allow you to figure out where your efficiencies and inefficiencies lie.

Establishing detailed reporting with accurate data can be a powerful tool when it comes to improving your processes. If you get all of that in place, you will be able to turn every mistake or even a crisis situation into an opportunity for your agency to become better.

This aspect is particularly important because identifying problems can be a big issue. Whenever something goes wrong, you might be unsure of whether it was due to an individual mistake or a fault in your processes. In that case, certain mishaps can pass unnoticed and sometimes even become a constant flaw in how your agency operates.

With proper information collecting and data reporting, you can make sure that you are always aware of exactly what happened. Then you can introduce a system that makes it impossible for the same mistake to happen again.

Finally, it is worth mentioning that the more complex your services become, the more chance errors will occur. That's why you should always be wary of creating an over-engineered service with too many moving parts. This kind of approach is precisely what leads to more waste accumulating, causing your processes to become inefficient in the long run.

When creating your systems, always aim for simplicity. When combined with detailed reporting, this will make everything your agency does streamlined and every part of your process easy to revisit and improve.

Track Your Time

Time tracking is certainly not the favorite activity in any agency. In fact, almost everyone hates doing it.

However, it is still one of the best ways to measure your processes and find flaws in them.

Now, tracking time might not seem connected to discovering flaws at first sight. Yet, it might be the most straightforward way to do so. If you notice that an excessive amount of time is being put into something that should only take 15 minutes, that's a clear red flag.

Without time tracking, certain flaws could go unnoticed for months or years. These do not necessarily have to be critical mistakes but can be flaws that cause your agency to gain less profit than it should.

In an example from one of our clients, the agency was seemingly working very well. They were satisfied with how much they were making by the hour, and the agency was always on budget.

However, a quick check of their stats revealed a shocking fact: the agency should've been about five times as profitable as it currently was.

After that discovery, the agency decided to take a closer look at their utilization. This was something they were not monitoring before.

Instead, the agency considered utilization based on how many hours a day people were working and how many hours they had logged. The agency's main focus was to ensure everything was within budget, and whenever someone was going out of budget, they would put it down to administrative time.

In this setup, it was no wonder that the agency was hitting their metrics – everyone in the company was trying to game the system, and their overall administrative time was 68%.

In other words, their project time wasn't as high as it should've been.

The solution was to find a system in which everyone's objectives were aligned. Of course, this couldn't happen overnight.

When you start time tracking and aligning, some fluctuations will inevitably happen before everything evens out. That's exactly what took place in this agency.

Their administrative time went down to between 8% and 15%, which was where they wanted it to be. However, the project time jumped because people still thought they needed to put in eight hours of work.

However, after the first 100 days, the situation started to even out. The process was initially somewhat turbulent, but once it settled, the rewards were easily worth it.

This example applies to most agencies. You might be happy with the overall profit margin and the results your agency is currently getting.

But once you start tracking time and working out where most of it is spent, you might find that some marginal processes are sapping profitability.

Time efficiency can help you extrapolate plenty of other data points that could increase efficiency. For example, suppose you have a high performer within your agency who's spending half of their time on the most profitable activities and the other half on low hourly rate tasks.

In that case, you might want to put someone else on the less profitable jobs to take that burden away from the high performer and effectively double their capacity.

The amount of applications for time tracking is astounding. One of our clients was able to add over $3.6 million of additional profit by doing a time study and accounting for the inefficiencies. Another client discovered one million dollars of waste with scheduling meetings and attending internal admin meetings.

When you start collecting time data, discovering potential opportunities for improvements, and applying the information gathered through tracking, you will find plenty of ways to make your processes considerably more efficient.

As a result, your agency will be able to deliver consistently and without getting overwhelmed. You will know how much time goes into getting particular results from every stage of a project. The bottom line is that time tracking will also help you adjust your pricing so that it reflects the actual amount of work that goes into your deliverables.

All things considered, once you start to track time and analyze it properly, it will be a revolutionary change to how your agency works. And when the benefits start coming in, you will find that the process was worth your while.

Effective Management Leads to Successful Projects

This chapter dealt mostly with the things you can do once you have already established a relationship with a client and started working with them. However, there is another factor that will decide your success, and that is whether or not you can choose the right clients to work with.

This is a key consideration that you should always keep in mind. You can spend years with the same client, and you will want to make sure that they are the kind of people that will inspire you and drive you forward.

When you choose your clients and start working with them, the overall success of your projects will largely depend on how well you manage them.

We have put a lot of emphasis on setting client expectations, and that will continue to play an important role throughout your relationship with them. It is imperative to make it clear what you will be delivering and where the boundaries are. If you do that right, your clients will know precisely what they will get, and you will reduce the chances of projects getting out of hand due to unrealistic requests and scope creep.

You will progress your relationship with clients even further if you pay attention to the fine details. On the one hand, the client needs to feel appreciated and know that you have their best interest in mind. On the other hand, you will need to learn to say no to certain requests, put a stop to doing recurring extra work outside of the original scope, and ensure that your clients understand when you do them a one-time favor.

From the inside perspective, you will need to set up processes to take care of scope creep, eliminate waste, and make your agency as efficient as possible.

All of these factors go into effective management. And if you can get them right, you will be able to guarantee success with almost every single project.

Gift #6 - Agency Profitability Analysis Guide

Want to find out which of your services, clients, and team members are the most profitable?

This guide walks you through the process of lining up each aspect of your agency to determine which areas need your attention most. With it, you can also pinpoint the areas that are draining the most resources and causing the greatest amount of waste.

You'll discover:

1. Effective billing rate: Learn the process for determining your actual effective billing rate across your agency. This provides you with a baseline of how to compare the price of each project to another.
2. Team Analysis: Discover step-by-step formulas for determining the profitability of your team. This analysis ensures that your best performers are not taking most of the workload, thus burning them out. It will also allow you to more effectively manage your team.

3. Project & Client Analysis: Do you know which projects and clients are most profitable? Once you identify them, you can pinpoint why they bring in the most profits. You can then make those projects more repeatable, making your agency more profitable.

4. Service Analysis: Which of your services contribute most to your profit? Armed with this information, you can focus on clients who need those particular services and create greater profitability in your agency.

Follow this link to download now: creativeagencysuccess.com/resources

CHAPTER 9

Hiring the Right People (and How to Set Them Up for Success)

Imagine a new person coming to work at an agency.

They go through all the usual stuff – meeting with HR, filling out the necessary paperwork, and all the rest of the motions.

So far, so good.

Then, the new employee meets the team member who is going to train them in all of the skills they will need for the job. They spend the first day of the training easing into their new roles and getting a basic grasp of how things work.

Things start getting more serious and much more challenging.

The trainer has at most three days to get the employee up to speed. By the end of the week, they are supposed to start working on client deliverables.

So the trainer offloads 50 million different things on the newcomer's head. The training seems a bit tough, but everything still looks alright.

And then, day four comes, and the new employee gets to work.

And all hell breaks loose.

The training wheels are off, and the work starts piling up all around them. All this leaves the employee feeling overwhelmed, and they become painfully aware that they cannot handle it.

By the end of the week, they already feel like they do not understand what they are supposed to do.

The very next Monday is gut-wrenching. The new employee is getting ready for five days of struggling, suffering, hair pulling, and feelings of ineptitude.

And while they're toiling beneath the growing frustration, the person who trained them cannot help but feel the same desperation.

This might sound like a horror story, but it is precisely what happens in most agencies when they onboard someone new. Of course, people get better progressively as they learn the processes, expectations, and culture of their workplace.

However, the first one to three months are all but guaranteed to be filled with stress for everyone involved. It is a miserable experience that takes way too much time. Besides all of the frustration, this common way of onboarding can cost the agency up to $15,000, and that is not even including the new employee's compensation.

Let's imagine a different scenario.

Again, we have a new employee who comes in, meets HR, and goes through all those initial steps.

Then, they start training.

Now, this person may have some previous experience with the usual onboarding process. So they hunker down and expect a torrent of information to come crashing down on them before they get thrown into the fray.

But that is not what happens.

The new employee spends the first week of their training learning about communication, technology, and systems. They get to know everything about how the agency functions and what the expectations are for the job.

After that first week, the employee starts feeling uneasy. They have spent all of that time without learning the actual skills that they will need to use.

The following Monday turns out not to be gut-wrenching. The new employee comes into work expecting to find themselves in the eye of the hurricane but is surprised to find a safe work environment.

The first thing they get is an explanation of the five non-negotiables – the five things that define success in their new job.

Then, for the next five weeks, they spend each week doing one of those nonnegotiables. And they do not only learn how to do them but how to excel at them.

Finally, the training period ends. Rather than an overwhelmed, frustrated employee who doesn't know what to do, the agency welcomes a confident new rockstar to its ranks.

The difference between the two approaches is massive. The streamlined, six-week training process results in a person making a decent start. This new team member will be able to expertly execute on the work; they won't need someone to hold their hand for months. Also, they typically stay in the positions for much longer and are vastly more successful in the position. The stress and frustration are minimized, and everyone is better at it.

Getting the right training process in place is undoubtedly one of the crucial aspects of onboarding, with another essential part being to choose the right people to hire.

In this chapter, we'll explain how to make the best possible decisions in that regard and ensure your agency has a winning team.

Defining Who You Need to Hire

Most agency owners do not start with a clear idea of who they need to hire. In fact, in the majority of cases, agency owners start off solo, and it might take some time before they even begin to consider building a team.

However, as your agency grows, the need for hiring new people will undoubtedly come. You might set out doing marketing, sales, delivery, and everything in between. And as you take so much ownership over your agency, the idea of bringing someone else in might become a challenge.

And yet, it will be necessary at some point.

The question will then become how to determine the right people for the job. And the answer will be in figuring out the four quadrants of all of the things you do within your agency.

The four quadrants consist of:

1. Your superpower – the thing you are absolutely the best at
2. Things you are good at
3. Something you can do okay
4. Things you cannot do well

How will these four quadrants help you define who you need to hire?

First, you will need to eliminate everything in your superpower. You will want to keep that thing you are amazing at for yourself. Then, look at the other three quadrants and hire for your weak points.

It might take some time to figure out which activity falls into which quadrant, but once you have the complete list, using it to find the right people to hire will be much more straightforward.

And the process will be that much easier if you follow the five principles of hiring.

The Five Principles of the Right Hire

1. Hire From the Bottom

The first hires you should make should never be for higher-level functions. Instead, you should start by filling out administrative and support roles.

This is because hiring strategists and creative direction people will be a much more challenging process. It will take a lot of time to find people to fill those roles, and they will be the most expensive ones. Essentially either adding an expense that you are not ready to make or delaying a hire that you need until you are drowning. Either way, not a good outcome.

2. Stop Trying to Replace You

This is a point we have covered in large part when talking about the four quadrants and finding your superpower. However, it is worth mentioning that this superpower is what makes you one of a kind, and that's something you will not be able to replace.

But when it comes to activities from other quadrants, you will find that other people can take up those roles. In fact, some might fit into certain positions better than you, and that is something you should view as an advantage.

Rather than replacing yourself, focus on finding people who can bring their unique experiences and imagination to expand and improve your agency.

3. Hire Slow and Fire Fast

While it is important to take your time when considering who to hire, it is equally important not to hold on to certain people for too long.

You can do everything right in the hiring process and still find yourself in a situation where the person you have hired turns out to be the wrong choice. If two or more months go by and you see their performance stay at a low level, the best thing to do will be to let that person go.

Keeping the wrong employee on board is much like asking for takeout food from a restaurant you didn't like. The food won't get any better – it will only make your refrigerator smell.

Whether you feel that keeping that employee is the right thing to do or you are hoping to be proven right, it will become a detriment to your goals.

4. Identify the Responsibilities

One of the first things you should let your employees know is what their role is and what good performance in that role looks like.

People want to be a part of the team, and they want to know that they're doing a good job without being micromanaged all the time. When you show them all of the responsibilities and expectations right from the start, they will understand precisely what they need to do and what goals they should achieve within your processes.

You want every employee to have a clear picture of what defines success and failure and be aware of it beyond any doubt.

5. Understand the Responsibility of Management

When you progress from a solo agency owner into someone managing a team, your responsibilities will change.

You will no longer be judged by your individual success. Instead, that will transfer to the success of the team you are managing, and that will entail a great number of things.

You will be responsible for managing your employees and their expectations, as well as representing your agency and managing its culture. You will also need to understand your team and communicate with them effectively.

As the head manager in your agency, you will have to provide your team with all of the necessary tools to enable them to achieve the best possible results.

Finally, and most importantly, make sure that you are inspiring your team and keeping them motivated and energized.

Stop Setting Your People Up for Failure – Learn How to Train

Here we come back with the very point that started this chapter: training.

As evident from our introductory story, the typical method of training and onboarding most often results in frustration and a failure to train new employees properly.

The other method described will all but guarantee superior results in that regard. However, it is crucial to cover several key aspects of your training process to ensure it is the most effective.

1. Do not assume that people know anything about your processes. Cover all of the details, including those that seem obvious.

2. Have standard operating procedures (SOPs) in place and prioritize training on those procedures.

3. If certain errors start appearing, fall back to the SOPs and retrain. Make sure to do this as soon as you notice an error in order to solidify the right procedures.

4. Maintain a knowledge bank for easy reference. This will streamline the training process and make it more straightforward.

5. Do not rely on linear training. Just because new team members have gone through it once doesn't mean the training is done. People usually retain about 70% of what they've learned and forget an additional 10%–15% over time. Always supply resources to fill in those knowledge gaps. Make those resources easily accessible.

6. Create a clear and repeatable training plan. Ideally, have the process automated to avoid mistakes or crucial points being left behind.

The Right People Allow for Quality Delivery

Creating the ideal team can be a long process that requires a great deal of care and attention. you will need to find the right people to fill in critical roles within your agency and bring improvements.

This process will rely on how well you can determine which roles you need to hire for first. Outlining the four quadrants will be of great help here as it will help you understand what the strongest and weakest points are.

Then, you will need to take your time in selecting the best candidates for specific positions. But that will not be the end of this process. you will have to adopt a foolproof method of training your team members to remove the usual stress and frustration and allow them to excel at their job the first day they finish training.

If you get all of this right and manage to put the right people in the right places, your agency will see massive improvements in its processes and delivery. Consequently, this will lead to better client satisfaction and growth.

Gift #7 - The Agency Blueprint – The Right Hire

Interested in learning more about how to hire and manage a team? Are you considering freelancers, nearshoring, or offshoring?

Download a free copy of Robert Patin's first book, *The Agency Blueprint*.

In this book, you'll find out:

1. Outsourcing/working with freelancers is often how many small agencies offload their work. And, more often than not, the first "hire." However, there are many considerations with this that are often missed by agency owners – from intellectual property rights, management, etc.

2. Nearshoring & offshoring are great ways to expand your workforce at lower costs. But there are certain factors to consider before taking the leap.

3. The right hire – making sure you have the right butts in the right seats – is a key component to successful agency management. When you are ready to make this happen, be sure that you have all contingencies considered.

Follow this link to download now: creativeagencysuccess.com/resources

CHAPTER 10

Consistent Results

There's a car manufacturer based in Florida that does something completely amazing.

Their name is Revology Cars, and they build classic Ford Mustang and Shelby models, ranging from the 1966 to 1968 series. But those cars are classic only at first sight.

Revology takes the well-known and loved shapes of the cars and places an entirely modern machine underneath. This means that their 1966 Mustang drives more like a contemporary sports car than an old-timer.

However, that's not all. The cars produced by this company are highly customizable. Every vehicle that comes out of Revology is unique, and the customer can choose between several options for almost every element of the car.

You can order a Revology Mustang with manual or automatic gear shifting, in custom colors, with unique wheels, dash, wheel, seat covers, carpets, and loads of other options.

All this sounds impressive and like a dream come true for classic Ford aficionados. However, there are limits to what you can get from Revology.

For instance, if you'd come to their store and say you'd like a '62 Corvette (beautiful car), the answer would be that the company doesn't make those. In fact, if you would ask for a 1969 Mustang, the reply would be the same.

You see, while the cars Revology puts out are fantastically customizable, their process is not. The process is rock-solid and highly standardized, and everyone who wants to buy a Revology car knows exactly what they can get.

This is a crucial aspect of the company; they will work wonders for their clients and produce 1966–1968 Mustang and Shelby models that are one of a kind. But that's where they will draw the line.

No one can get a car from Revology for which they do not have a process – the company simply will not do it.

This is because the company has an established process and a repeatable service that allows them to get consistent results every time.

And you can achieve the same within your agency by following certain key guidelines, which we'll explore in this chapter.

How to Create Consistent Results

"If you want to impress people, make things complicated. If you want to help them, keep it simple."

– Frank Kern

Creating an environment that allows for consistent results is always a step in the right direction. When your clients know that they can expect you to deliver your services with the same level of quality, they will always be eager to work with your agency.

Furthermore, consistent results lead to overall happier clients. This, in turn, leads to repeat revenue. In other words, once you establish that consistency, you will be able to produce the best results every time and allow your agency to grow unhindered.

Before we get into a detailed explanation of what your process should consist of, there's one point we need to clarify.

Creatives often have an objection when it comes to the ideas of process and repetition. In particular, they fear that focusing on those aspects will take away from the creativity in their agency. However, that fear is unfounded.

To put it simply, it's not an either/or proposition. Achieving process and repetition doesn't mean that creativity has to be sacrificed or sidelined. When done right, your agency can create a productive synergy between these seemingly oppositional goals. Having a consistent, repeatable process streamlines the logistical and administrative burden of your business processes – thus creating more space for creativity, innovation, improvisation, and exploration.

In an ideal scenario, you achieve the best of both worlds. You will be able to *consistently* provide your clients with the results they need, rather than placing your faith in unpredictable flashes of creative genius. Creativity will always stay at the core of your agency – the process will simply make it easier to deliver your creative work in the most satisfying way for your clients.

Here are the essential steps to follow if you want to create consistent results that enhance your agency's creative potential:

1. Productize Your Services

Productizing your services means having service packages that function in a very specific way to help your clients accomplish their goals. You will only be able to do this if you cover all of the basics concerning your service:

- Ensure it is something that your target demographic really needs.
- Know and deliver that service exceptionally well.
- Create a service that drives results.
- Have an intricate understanding of the process behind delivering your service.

Today's agency space is absolutely bombarded with people who have nothing more than a laptop. They watch a couple of YouTube videos and get convinced that they suddenly know how to run Facebook ads or do SEO.

Those people get out into the market certain that they've become digital ad buyers, and this completely destroys the industry. Making prospects mistrust the next agency they encounter, making it harder to help them.

The fact of the matter is that you need to be an expert in what you are talking about. You must know what you are doing inside out to generate results.

This is the basic foundation for scaling.

It is also the main reason why so many agencies fail at delivering results. They try to be everything to everyone only to get new leads and clients. Then, they push themselves into doing projects that they've never done before and hope that they will learn it along the way, ironing out (inevitable) unexpected setbacks as they go.

The issue is that entire agencies continue to grow on that foundation, becoming generalists that cannot deliver value consistently.

If you want to grow your agency in a better way, you need to decide what your primary service is before you start offering it. Then, you should tell people exactly what it is that you do, as well as what you do not do.

Furthermore, you should ensure that you are delivering your service in one fashion. You might have different package types, but they should be based on the same set of things you can do effectively.

This approach will affect how well you can scale your agency, how much time you are focusing on delivering, and the amount of work that you need to do with each client. More than that, it will affect your client satisfaction and retention and your ability to sell.

Productize your services, and it will define your business in many ways.

2. Build a Repeatable Process

This step might sound simple. If you want your agency to scale, you need a process that's scalable.

Think about the Revology company we have talked about in the introduction. They create unique, custom products through a process that obviously doesn't allow them to serve everyone on the planet. That company couldn't make a million cars within a year because it would take too much time and resources.

However, their strength lies in a repeatable process that produces the same level of results every time. That's precisely what your agency needs.

You should have a package that's plug-and-play. There might be slight variations from one client to the other, but those will be limited to changing one piece of your offer for another. In those cases, all you will need to do will be simple transfers that will remain within your scope.

You can create different packages inside of your repeatable process by making templates that can be layered on top of each other.

For example, you can have package A which has a particular list of services. Then, you have package B that covers everything from A and layers some extra services on top of it. Finally, your package C could include both A and B, along with another layer of other services.

The main advantage of this approach is that you will be able to offer different options to your clients without adding too much complexity to your processes.

Automation can be of great help in this regard. There's so much technology today that you can leverage to get different parts of your process to fire in an instant, saving plenty of time and ensuring repeatable results.

3. Be Iterative

Being iterative goes back to the point we raised in the previous chapter, and it is about adjusting your process to account for potential errors.

This is a change that you can introduce on a system level whenever a mistake happens within your process or when a particular area could be improved for better performance.

Ensuring that your processes are iterative will allow you to optimize everything for the future. This is something to keep in mind when you start building your processes. They need to be flexible enough so that certain parts can be adjusted without rebuilding the process from scratch.

Of course, new technology can be a great asset when it comes to improvements, and so can the ideas that come from your team. Team members will often have ground knowledge and valuable insight that comes from it. That's why you should always consult your team when deciding on which changes to introduce.

When we talk about being iterative, you should bear in mind that the principle also applies to your standard operating practices. Being able to adapt your SOPs to new circumstances will play a significant role in producing results more consistently.

4. Understand That There's Comfort in Data

Creativity might be the driving force behind your agency, but it is important to accept that it has its limits. This is especially true when it comes to standardizing your services and deliverables and tracking various metrics for efficiency.

People in the creative industry can get used to making decisions based on instinct. However, while that instinct may prove true or false, numbers never lie. In other words, it is useful to have certainty through data.

It is much easier to make decisions when you have empirical data on things like time management, client satisfaction, efficiency, or other metrics. This is precisely why it is important to acknowledge the limitations of creativity and put your trust in data when making improvements or adjustments to your systems.

Everything that affects how you deliver your service or the results for your clients and agency should be based on data; every good creative knows the value of instincts and feelings, but acknowledging that even these have limits is critical to success.

While this seems understandable on its own, many people believe that they already know everything they need to know and think they do not have to research relevant information. Making a gut decision will more likely leave you awake at night, wondering whether you did the right thing. But if you make decisions based on information, data, and knowledge, you will feel much more comfortable.

5. Cool Doesn't Matter if It Doesn't Sell

Abandoned showrooms and basements are full of cool ideas that nobody wants to buy. And this is not something limited to small inventions. Industry giants can often mistake cool for salable.

Back in 2004, the Coca-Cola company tried to enter the U.K. market with their bottled water brand, Dasani.

This brand has been wildly successful so far. In fact, Dasani is still the second-best bottled water in the world regarding sales. With a product that's performed that well, Coca-Cola didn't have any doubts about its success in the British market.

They introduced Dasani with all of the fanfare and promotional bells and whistles you could imagine, with the company backing up the marketing campaign with millions of pounds.

But the British public wasn't impressed.

The initial reception was lukewarm, and it grew colder after certain facts about Dasani water came out.

Coca-Cola's bottled water turned out not to be sourced from a natural spring. It was actually purified tap water.

Despite all of the cool marketing and branding, as well as one of the world's largest companies providing ample support for their product, Dasani failed to sell in the U.K. It took no more than a few weeks for the bottled water to be recalled, never to return to the British Isles.

This is just one example that shows that people aren't willing to stick with a product or service if it doesn't work for them. You can make it sound like the coolest thing ever, and it might even sell very well initially.

However, if what you are selling doesn't resonate with your audience, they will not return for the same thing again. Additionally, you will not get any new leads from those clients.

6. Remove Subjectivity and Track Everything

If you want to ensure that your processes are repeatable and provide consistent results, it would be best to leave nothing open to interpretation or chance.

The way you structure processes within your agency should be as objective as possible. Once you establish those, tracking all relevant metrics will help you determine efficiency and opportunities for improvements.

When it comes to making repeatable processes, checklists can be a surprisingly effective tool. In fact, hospitals in the U.S. famously use checklists for various scenarios, from regular maintenance and standard procedures to responding to infection outbreaks.

Using checklists to back up your processes will ensure that you get the same results every time because you will need to perform the same actions to tick each box. Additionally, having a visual representation of the process will help you better organize time and individual responsibilities.

To further expand on the objectiveness and repeatability, you should document your standard operating procedures. SOPs should describe every step within a particular procedure to allow your team to deliver results in the same way.

As you want to document your SOPs in the most understandable way possible, follow this three-part outline when writing them down:

1. Start with a description outlining the SOP in broader terms.
2. Layout the instructions for specific steps and actions that go into the procedure.
3. List the references and additional material that could be of further use.

Document the SOPs so that they're clear and understandable, and do not forget to update them whenever significant changes are introduced.

Keeping your SOPs concise and updated will be of great help for your team, both in terms of repeatable results and when it comes to onboarding new members.

Once you get the system in place, you should track everything to get the most extensive data on the effectiveness of your processes. Here, technology will be key.

7. *Building Knowledge*

You can leverage technology to great advantage in various areas like automation, information transference, communicating with clients, generating results, and reliable reporting.

Agency owners often spend too much time doing agency work without paying attention to new solutions constantly coming up in the industry. Unfortunately, this can mean that pieces of technology that could be crucial for your agency are going unnoticed.

If you want to stay on top of novel solutions, one of the best ways to do so would be to talk about it with other people in your industry.

There's a misguided mindset that, just because agencies are in the same industry, they have to act like competitors and foster a kind of "frenemies" relationship. You should definitely remove this mindset and start connecting with other agency owners and people who share your space.

There are 320,000+ creative and marketing agencies in the U.S. alone and millions of potential clients. There's no reason to think that you and other agency owners are stepping on each other's toes. In fact, from our experience working with countless clients on countless pitches, we have only ever encountered clients pitching the same client twice. It would be best to establish and grow your relationships so that you can learn about new tools, technology, and ways to innovate. These interactions will prove priceless when it comes to improving the way your agency works.

Set Yourself Up for Success

In terms of delivering results, consistency will be paramount. Learning how to set up your processes to get the same results every single time will be one of the most valuable things for the future of your agency.

It cannot be overstated how important it is to make your delivery repeatable. While individual projects will always be somewhat different, you will be able to account for those variations much easier when you have an established way of doing things.

Many aspects of your agency will depend on consistent delivery. With wellestablished, repeatable processes, you will have a better grasp of the scope of projects. You will have a clear outline of what results your agency can produce and everything that goes into getting those results.

Setting clear client expectations improves satisfaction, making it easier to grow your agency. And once that starts happening, you will have no problems scaling your processes because you have established them the right way.

This brings us to the end of this book.

You now know a bit more about who we are, what we do, and what our goals are. Namely, we want to help you succeed in the fastest way possible. That's why, chapter by chapter, we went through the three critical aspects of creating an efficient and profitable agency.

First, you learned what it takes to attract the right clients by selecting your niche, specializing, and marketing in the most effective way.

For the second aspect, we moved on to converting prospects into clients and described the complete sales process. This included everything from determining which type of salesperson you are, through the discovery calls, to mastering the art of the close.

Finally, we looked at ways to ensure your delivery is always top-quality with fantastic, repeatable results that will help you retain plenty of satisfied clients.

Now, all that's left is for you to start adopting the right mindset that will drive your agency to success. All of the key factors are clear, and they're ready for you to use them. Of course, building up your agency will take time, much planning, and careful deliberation. But then, the best things in life often do.

www.ingramcontent.com/pod-product-compliance
Lightning Source LLC
Chambersburg PA
CBHW060422220526
45465CB00008B/2976